worlds within worlds

worlds within worlds

Ajay Navaria

Translation of the Hindi novel *Udhar ke Log* by

Nita Kumar

THORNBIRD

NIYOGI BOOKS

Published by
NIYOGI BOOKS
Block D, Building No. 77,
Okhla Industrial Area, Phase-I,
New Delhi-110 020, INDIA
Tel: 91-11-26816301, 26818960
Email: niyogibooks@gmail.com
Website: www.niyogibooksindia.com

Editor: Vibha Chakravarty Kumar
Design: Shashi Bhushan Prasad
Cover design: Misha Oberoi

ISBN: 978-93-91125-80-6
Publication: 2024

Price: ₹495

Printed at Niyogi Offset Pvt. Ltd., New Delhi, India

For my Dalit colleagues:
Mira, Pushpa, Rani, Kanti, and Chinta
With respect and affection

Contents

Foreword

What are these worlds within worlds?

I want to begin a discussion of the novel strategically with the wedding, spread over Chapters 7 (Towards the Wedding), 8 (The Ritual Lunch), 9 (Ayesha's Style), 10 (Weber Arrives) and 11 (We Friends). Rinku, the younger brother of the protagonist—narrator, Masterji, is getting married. In the course of the five days or so of the wedding, we read about the devious yet innocent plot of Masterji to get his estranged wife Sangita back. We read about prolonged wedding rituals—including different family members' roles, the abusive ritual songs sung by women, and the lunch at which the man and woman's families are (ritually) at the opposite sides and come together. We go into deep discussions about caste and untouchability. We learn of the prostitute Ayesha's quest to be a normal member of a family and society. We have intense scenes of male bonding with heart-to-heart conversations about sex, manhood and power. Finally, we share the author-narrator's musing on modernisation in India and the growing popularity of 'Punjabi' culture; on the meaning of family and community; and on the importance of education.

This platter of topics covered gives an idea that what *Worlds within Worlds* partly is, is an education. The discussions about caste and hierarchy are informed by inside knowledge—and thus, deliberately informative. The wedding songs are almost ethnographic in style, the author taking an obvious pleasure in celebrating songs that many would consider trivial but we are invited not to. Because the narrator-protagonist is a soul-searching intellectual, we accompany him on his journey on the quest for the *truth* about hierarchy, patriarchy, oppression, community, the individual, love and friendship.

So intense are these different loci of education, as I am calling them, that we almost cannot digest the information all at once. Is Navaria deliberate and planned in his presentation of pages of wedding rituals to us between gatherings of Masterji and his friends to discuss agitatedly, over whiskey and beer, about the seeming irresolvable debates of caste and untouchability? Or is he doing it unreflectively, collapsing the author into the narrator?

Let us leave the author's intentions aside for the moment, and simply ruminate on what is achieved. What is achieved is a great levelling.

You can fight back the oppressor in many different ways. Of all the different ways, Navaria chooses the following: quietly be yourself. But show that you are as complex and differentiated, as clever and unfathomable, as deep-rooted and interesting, as problematic and political—as anyone out there that you are being, or may be, compared with. There is *not a trace* of victimhood or pitifulness here. Let us look at the five or six main plot lines of the novel through a focus on the wedding chapters, and the lens of the main characters—Amma, Papa, Sangita, Ayesha, and Masterji himself. We will also look at some sub-themes and the wonderful cast of secondary characters, mainly, Sushil, Jayant, Vedprakash, Aslam, Firoz, Rana, Kalra and Banwarilal.

Masterji's Schemes and a Big Fat Wedding

First, we have the plot of Masterji trying to win back his estranged wife Sangita. When he married her, he failed to share with her the information that he was not just already married before, but that his first wife had committed suicide. He had then gone to jail for six months on the basis of her posthumous note, accusing him of alcoholism and wife beating. When Sangita finds out, she walks out of their house and refuses to talk to him. She remains close to his grandmother, Amma, and agrees to attend his brother Rinku's wedding. During the course of some two days—she only comes on the final days—

Masterji tries every ploy to win her back: from talking to her in heartfelt ways and pitting her against the exemplary beauty Ayesha, to encouraging all his friends and family members to plead on his behalf. Does she relent? Masterji thinks to himself, 'It seems my plot is working.' Just a few minutes later, 'That didn't work…'

A second plot-line, and one that has a totally different panoramic dimension, is that of the wedding activities. Now, in this rather typical Indian wedding, nothing actually *happens* except 'the usual'. There are rituals, overladen with meanings ascribed to them privately and publicly. There are the intrigues and family gossip, in turn dictated not only by histories but by personalities. It's a veritable *Monsoon Wedding* scenario—and for anyone who knows India, exceedingly familiar. We are first explained the *haldi*, or turmeric, ritual, designed to make the bride and groom's bodies shine at their best. We are reminded about this ritual time and again as it comes to be used as an instrument to make Sangita stay on and become embroiled in family affairs, or as it allows Ayesha to also participate as if she were an insider. It is hardly an innocent ritual but rather a useful tool; as Masterji muses, 'Man makes rituals and then finds himself caught in their webs.'

Then there are the wedding songs at every turn. Several anthropologists (especially Raheja and Gold 1994, but see also Kumar 1992, Banerjee 1989) have documented and interpreted these songs in their historical and social contexts, and it is wonderful to see them lodged comfortably within the frame of a novel. Predictably, Ayesha, the call girl, treats them as performative pieces; younger women from the village or the 'community' sing them un-reflectively as familiar wedding appendages; older women show off their storehouse of knowledge; reform-minded or quieter women like Amma want to do away with them; men simply ignore them. Masterji observes. He is interested in neither their lyrics nor their melody, but only in what Ayesha or Sangita do with them. Once again, a seemingly innocent practice is a weapon depending on participation.

The *bhat* is a ritual lunch where *kachcha,* or uncooked—more correctly, non-fried—food is served by the bride's side to the bridegroom's party, thus incorporating them in the community defined by sharing such food, a community to which they did not belong previously. In this novel, the *bhat* occurs before the wedding, and the two sides consist of the bridegroom's maternal and paternal relatives. The mother is the fulcrum, having left her natal home—specifically her brothers and their families (her parents are no more)—and become part of her conjugal home, her husband, his mother, his sisters. The family is sizeable and follows all the traditional procedures in full. The gift-giving from one side to the other, the emotions evoked by visitors and transactions, then the re-presentation of the action as performance, in song and movement, are all part of the plot.

Then comes the wedding procession, or *barat*. We linger over the bridegroom getting ready, over the departure of the bridegroom's party and the separate departure of Masterji with his friends, and the song and dance that follows. There is an 'Indian wedding syndrome' perhaps summarised in the dictum 'the more chaos, the merrier', and it is followed fully in this particular wedding. So much so that when a friend who missed it comes the next day and asks how it went, no one can think of a fitting reply.

On the final day while everyone is resting—including the bride and the groom—and gossiping, including about dowry, we have a quick mention of the substantial gifts given by the bride's family: clothes, jewellery, furniture, car *and cash*. It is enough to silence the aunt who went around wagging her tongue about what was wrong with the whole alliance of Rinku and Suman. Although the father of the groom is against taking dowry, he does not say a word; and this is smoothly explained by one of the aunts, 'Well, it's good of him to say no, but should the girl's side take the no seriously? If they were to give a dowry, would we refuse?' Indeed, it is not refused. Interestingly, while the father and the grandmother—the virtuous people in the story—remain silent about it, Masterji, an obsessive social commentator who sees sociological and political explanations behind every personal act, has not a word to say on the subject.

The Business of Caste, and the Questions about Education

The third, terribly important thread followed in the wedding chapters as well as the whole novel is about the predominance of caste hierarchies.

Now, a word about caste. We can understand caste in two broad ways: as structure and as culture. As structure, it would be all-encompassing, a mechanical system, or a web, into which every member of society fits (through their groups, not as individuals). As culture, it is also all-encompassing, but works in decentred, unitary ways. Thus, every caste has its culture, to some extent unrelated to the culture of other castes. Additionally, as culture at an abstract level, the very meaning of caste depends on a belief in concepts of purity and pollution, high and low, left and right, substance and code.

The author presents caste as both structure and culture. The novel's caste structure is that of a ladder, and the ladder is almost infinitely regressive. At every rung, there are other rungs below. You may or may not know who are at the furthest rungs, but you certainly know who are at several rungs directly above and below you. Rather, you *think* you know—as everything else, caste has a history, and the history is a multiple one of many versions. So, one caste's claimed position is another caste's falsehood.

What Navaria narrates is an ongoing set of discussions among Masterji and his friends, Sushil, Jayant, Vedprakash, Rana, and Kalra, with the Muslim friends listening on, and some others included occasionally in their convivial parties. These discussions are not at rallies or meetings, they do not attend acts of atrocity and violence, they are not grounded in tragedy. On the contrary, they are accompanied by whiskey and beer, back slapping and teasing friendship, heavy male bonding, and an underlying echo of success. Sushil is a Deputy Commissioner of Police. Jayant is also (after repeated tries) in the Indian Police Service. The other three are powerful executives. Masterji is a respected tenured lecturer at a public university. Everyone has a job, a house, a car, self-respect, and an equality with anyone in a democratic society. They are all educated. Caste should not matter.

But it does. Sushil is of Bhangi caste, which had the traditional occupation of cleaning latrines and gutters. Renamed after the author of the *Ramayana* as Valmiki (or Valmiki), Sushil's caste is regarded as 'untouchable' even by other 'untouchable' castes. Not a politically correct term any longer, it can best be used now to sneer, protest, accuse, and deny. Jayant is of Chamar caste, renamed Jatav, which had the traditional job of skinning and working with leather. Sushil protests that his caste, Bhangi/Valmiki, has been and continues to be trodden upon and marginalised by Jayant's caste, Chamar/Jatav. Indeed Sushil, more than once, equates Chamar with Brahman in the caste hierarchy as it is experienced. For Bhangis, Chamars are as much the enemy as Brahmans are. Indeed, Brahmans may typically be absent from Dalits' lives, but Dalits are always present for one another. Insofar as that they seem one united, identifiable group form the outside, they are, so to speak, stuck with each other. Never mind the details of who is above you. If they are above you, you and they are enemies and since they consistently practice this enmity, it behoves you to practise it too.

Masterji is Khatik by caste, traditionally related to the occupations of butchering animals and removing carcasses. The novel does not make it clear but Khatik are above Bhangi/Valmiki and under, or on par, with Chamar/Jatav. We see that at Rinku's wedding, Rinku's *mamis* (maternal uncles' wives), whose traditional family role is to throw barbs at their husband's sister, ask sneeringly if Rinku's bride is a Chamar. They are told she is a Khatik, but are not fully reassured because her Khatik caste is a different sub-caste to theirs. Before the wedding, Amma, the grandmother, and the mother had the same worry—they were making an alliance 'out of caste'. All it was, was a sub-caste that had become differentiated from their own sub-caste through vagaries of history.

Khatiks swear by education as the panacea for the ills of caste discrimination, and share Bhim Rao Ambedkar's faith in democracy and the Constitution. Again and again, Masterji argues in his friends' circle that the path of education, followed by competitive examinations and success, is open to all. His friends demonstrate, one to all, the power of education. Their parents cleaned latrines and gutters, worked in traditional 'untouchable' occupations, remained in name, image, identity, low down and despised in the caste ladder. Their old village or city neighbourhoods were characterised as 'dirty' and were often the target of upper caste venom and violence. In the cities and in new surroundings, the new generation has merged smoothly into different echelons of middle-class life. They can joke now about cleaning gutters and being forced into unpaid labour.

The nightmare of untouchability, as we know it from elsewhere, is not revealed in the wedding chapters, but elsewhere. In Chapter 3, Masterji and Ayesha are just getting to know each other and consolidating their new friendship. This is part of the exchange:

> 'That Rana, however, he is a devil, the bastard.' She smiled and winked, and in that wink, transformed into another Ayesha.
>
> 'Why?' I stared at her in surprise.
>
> 'That bastard has...' She showed a size with her fingers and smiled. 'This is how these Doms are.'

I was at a loss. I could not decide if she was praising us or bad-mouthing us, whether to be pleased or not.

'Is Rana a Dom?'

'Of course...Scheduled castes are Doms, aren't they,' she said simply, and sipped her coffee.

I knew that Rana was not a Dom. He was a Dhanuk by caste and always called himself higher than Valmikis. I was silent...

She paused. 'These Doms are very dirty.'

'How do you know?' I stoked my anger.

'I've seen their homes in the village...Just as you did not let the beggar touch you near the flyover, that's how they are, filthy and smelly.' She waved the fly away. 'You can look at the fly but you can't swallow it, can you, Masterji?'

I thought of my village, where my own community lived in a dirty way. Most of them were poor, hard-working people. The one or two families that were well-off lived with pomp. What Ayesha was ascribing to caste was actually just about money.

'We are a high caste, Masterji.' She showed me the conch shell and red bangles on her wrist. She touched her gold bangle. It may have been gold or just brass. I could not keep my attention off the fly that continued to hover around us. 'We are Raychaudhuris. Ayesha Raychaudhuri.' Her voice had pride.

> I was nauseated to see this traditional pride on Ayesha's face. I felt like shouting at her, 'You bitch, you cheap prostitute. Here is another Dom standing in front of you to whom you are ready to swear devotion.'

We know that the practice of untouchability is arguably the most nightmarish of all practices. Article 17 of the Constitution of India states:

> Untouchability is abolished and its practice in any form is forbidden. The enforcement of any disability arising out of untouchability shall be an offence punishable in accordance with the law.

In addition, the Fundamental Rights (Part III) and the Directive Principles of State Policy (Part IV) incorporated in the Constitution clearly direct the state to protect and provide for the welfare of weaker sections. However, despite multiple constitutional safeguards, over seven decades after Independence and 33 years after the *Scheduled Castes and Scheduled Tribes Prevention of Atrocities Act 1989* (*SC/ST PoA Act*), Dalits still face discrimination, and fatal crimes—called 'atrocities'—against them are still reported. Many, particularly in the villages, live painful lives in the shadow of fear and humiliation. In 'Shining India':

> Every day, four *dalit* and *adivasi* (tribal) women are raped while 11 *dalits* and *adivasis* are beaten up. Every week, 13 *dalits* and *adivasis* are murdered, five *dalit* and *adivasi* homes are set on fire and six *dalits* and *adivasis* are kidnapped' (Mahim Pratap Singh, 'Untouched by Justice', *The Hindu*, 25 January 2013, p. 6; also see Khobragarde 2014: pp. 12-13.)

Worlds within Worlds has two mentions of atrocities against Dalits: one is an actual incendiary activity that the protagonist and his friend rush to, and second is the reference to such an activity. There are also references to camps put up by Dalit doctors in *basti*s. The *basti*, or poor neighbourhood, has the resonance in the novel of an undescribed pit of problems, if not hell. It must be escaped, for survival and sanity.

Then there is violence in the highest echelons. The best example is the killing of a Dalit Police officer, Birpal Singh Jatav, under the mask of an encounter with criminals so that it would seem that he had been killed by one of them. However, it was a government bullet that had killed him; and the Inspector who fired it confessed in front of the Search Committee that he could not tolerate hearing abuses from a Dalit, or washing the dirty dishes of a Dalit. This is something experienced routinely by all juniors from their seniors—but in all other cases the seniors were, and are, upper caste.

None of this turns out to be as disturbing as picking up a professedly Dalit novel, you might think it should be. The weight of Dalit-ness is borne lightly by Masterji and his friends. The author uses broad strokes when describing the past. In the present, the friends merely talk about the politics of discrimination and revenge; how, for instance, one is not invited to parties by those of another sub-caste (a friend comments that it's because of his own rude behaviour). All the emancipatory steps taken by Masterji and his friends, however, were originally conceptualised and pushed forward by their parents. About Sushil, we are told in Chapter 5, 'Vandana, Gone':

> Sushil's full name was Sushil Valmiki. His father had passed away when he was eleven or twelve years old. He worked as a sanitary worker in the City Municipality; and while cleaning the sewers one day, he had died. His wife had been given his job at the Municipality on compensatory grounds. Papa had helped them too. Because she was a woman, Sushil's mother had got a street sweeper's job.
>
> Educated till class X, Sushil's mother had grown up in this very city and was not prepared to take it. She did not want to sweep the streets. Her father worked in the Municipality as well, as a doorman. Her father and mine did some running around on her behalf, and finally she was appointed as a water woman.

> 'If it's the work that gives us the label of "dirty", then why do that work?' she says till today. 'Clean up the city and make *yourself* "dirty"; that's what's bringing the community down.'

Sushil's mother's matter-of-fact ideology may rankle with those who want more radical action. In this respect the novel seems the voice of Liberal Reason. It does not engage with any hand wringing. For the main protagonist, to talk about caste is to also talk about the social mobility possible through education. It is to talk about the discrimination practised all up and down the ladder, and the exclusivism at each rung. It is to ask each other with blame, 'Who is responsible for making this damn system? Your ancestors, not mine!' Vandana, one of the three upper caste characters in the novel, is told precisely this when she complains that her father-in-law is 'casteist' because he does not talk to her. He is, in fact. The other, Vedprakash, one of the group of Masterji's close friends, demonstrates enormous insensitivity. Sushil tells Masterji that Vedprakash, a Brahman, despises him for being a Valmiki. Then Vedprakash reveals as much. Finally, there is Ayesha, who remains somewhat of a mystery in that she is not called out ever for *her* overt caste-based prejudices. But she also spends five days in the bosom of a Dalit family and does not seem to recognise them as Dalits, or has closed her eyes to it because she would rather have a family and a friend than none at all.

Caste consciousness is voiced chiefly by Sushil and Jayant, a Valmiki/Bhangi and Jatav/Chamar, respectively. Sushil's complaint is that there cannot be progress until there is unity, and unity is an impossible goal since Jatavs are against Valmikis. Jayant's defence is that Jatavs have merely followed Ambedkar's teaching to the full: to organize, get an education, and get good jobs. The strategy has worked. Why would Valmikis not do that, instead of fighting to preserve their low-caste jobs?

Sushil feels that this is a Brahmanical argument—he claims at more than one place in the book that Jatavs have become equivalent to Brahmans. For Sushil, the promotion of education (although he is himself a direct beneficiary) is an argument that silences protest and advices acceptance of the status quo. At best, it blames the victim, expecting them to pull themselves up by their boot straps. The debate continues from the beginning to the end of the novel: if one group of Dalits have united successfully to fight off marginalisation, can other Dalits not be expected to do the same? Or is the fight against injustice doomed unless there is help from outside: from the government, from other castes?

Masterji is an observer to this. He is not passive, in that he routinely joins in the conversation. His position is clear, however. He avoids extremes. He silences angry eruptions. He warns against provocative pronouncements and derogatory remarks. He comments when people are making these in the grips of their third or later drink.

In Masterji we are presented with an exemplary portrait of a thoughtful intellectual who questions at every turn dualistic divisions, poorly researched conclusions, illiberal ideologies, and fanatical, sentimental and superficial statements. He comes across as quiet and sensitive. He does not suffer, except when he loses Sangita, and when he shares Ayesha's problems—but we can recognise all this as part of the intellectual's role. He is repeatedly accused by Sushil for being indirect in his critique of casteism, and for being soft on upper caste, including Jatavs—perhaps, Masterji speculates, because he (Masterji) married a Brahman, followed by a Khatik.

The biggest trump card for education comes from an unexpected source, *bua*, the paternal aunt (father's sister) who is right in the bosom of the caste-based community and family. Sangita announces that Masterji has lied in claiming Ayesha to be her (Sangita's) friend when she is in fact *his* friend. We all expect bua to be conservative in this matter—a married man's unannounced woman friend? Bua, however, says coolly,

> Such friendships are permitted in educated homes, you know. There are no caste or community people here to gossip. If the caste neighbourhood was around us, you would never hear the

> end of this friendship. There are some plus points to education, even if there are some minus ones.

Bua leaves without waiting for a response and Masterji adds to Sangita, 'Whatever they think, they will stand by me. They are my people.' He draws, as is done elsewhere too, a fine line between the immediate extended family that is loyal to its members, and the sub-caste or *biradari*, that speaks with an authoritarian voice and will never give you privacy or choice or identity.

Dirt/Flies and Colour/Complexion

Two important sub-themes in the book are: the presence of flies in unexpected places, and their metaphoric use for unacceptable filth; and the colour white, as well as fair, shining and golden complexions.

Flies are tolerated. They can be swiped away or waved away. They keep coming back but do not have to be touched. Then they fall into a cup of coffee. However, as Ayesha and Vedprakash, the two important upper caste characters in the novel, both say independently of each other at different times, 'Once you see it, you can't swallow it, can you?' They are describing their repugnance for lower castes. Dalits—called variously Chamars, Bhangis and Doms by the relatively ignorant—are claimed to be 'dirty', and therefore, repulsive.

Vedprakash does not mind Masterji, although he takes pains to point out that back in his village Masterji's caste, Khatik, was not one he would transact with. Ayesha does not mind Masterji, although, as quoted above, she says with a naiveté bordering on stupidity that Doms are dirty. Masterji, equating himself with a Dom in the spirit of her remark, ruminates about how his caste members back in the village do indeed live in dismally dirty conditions. Because they are *poor*, he insists. What is mistaken for a caste characteristic is simply the trait of poverty.

As for colour, the most outstanding case is that of Rana, who, from the beginning of the novel to the end, will wear only white, and drives a white car. Masterji asks him rather naively, first, if he has clothes of no other colour. Then, did he always like white, even when he was young? Then, if he is making up for being poor back in his village. He is explained curtly that when Rana was young, back in his village, someone of his caste could get a thrashing if they wore white. *Only* Brahmans could wear white. It was *not* a question of poverty versus wealth; the Brahman could be among the poorest, his clothes the most threadbare. So, once Rana got himself an education and a position, and acquired wealth and status, he chose to wear only white. Masterji is clearly out of the loop. His friends tell him that he is 'from the city', and that he is over-liberal and clueless.

Many people are fair complexioned in the novel. One of them is Masterji's brother, Rinku, the one getting married. We are told that he has inherited his mother's fair skin, whereas the rest of the family is sallow—so we know in a casual way that family members can have assorted complexions. Ayesha is fair, and her skin is radiant after a bath and a touch of turmeric at the pre-wedding rituals. Sangita, on meeting her, calls her 'like Marilyn Monroe'. Rinku, on the wedding night, Ayesha's fairness accentuated by golden jewellery, calls her 'an angel' and 'just like Aishwarya Rai', a fair-complexioned Beauty Queen and Bollywood star. She herself is hyper-conscious of her complexion, and after her association with the European, Weber, seems to be even more aware of whiteness.

Both the use of flies and the use of white are techniques that universalise the fact of caste difference and discrimination, while revealing to us the pain of those at the receiving end of the transaction.

The Prostitute and the Men (Dalit) Friends

How do we understand the drinking and whoring that goes on throughout the novel? It starts literally on the first few pages, with Masterji and Ayesha choosing between whiskey and beer, to Masterji's flashback as he remembers his first meeting with her. She has just had sex with Rana, downed a glass of whiskey in one gulp sitting with Kalra, and then goes into a closed room with Masterji to seduce him. She undoes her robe to reveal her lovely, naked body. He does not touch her, lectures her on her unholy profession, and their friendship is born. Why, he muses, as he goes home, could he not touch her? Surely not because she is not chaste… he remembers an earlier affair he has had with a married woman…The point about men's double standards—tolerate some un-chaste women but not others—is echoed towards the end of the book when Rana complains about his wife's infidelity, and how he feels nauseated by her now that she has been touched by another.

At that meeting, Masterji's friends Kalra and Rana, and at many later ones, his even better friends Sushil and Aslam, and sometimes Firoz and Jayant, refer to Ayesha as *randi, rakhail, cheez, kutiya, sali, haramzadi, vaishya* (a prostitute; someone's mistress or kept woman; an object; a bitch; a fucker ((literally, sister-in-law)); an illegitimate, despicable woman; a whore)—that is to say, in a no-holds-barred abusive language. We are surprised that Masterji, during the wedding, not only gets away with having her stay in his family for four or five days, but successfully defends her against public outrage by insisting she is a friend and a guest. To those who do not know her, she is introduced as 'a social worker in an NGO', and to others she is simply off-limits. Obviously, he has a lot of social leverage in his circles, and any doubts we may harbour as to why are partially allayed by Kalra's chance voice of sobriety, echoed by other friends, that Masterji is respectable, stable, balanced and the most educated of them all, and therefore, a kind of beacon for them. His soft power is such that, partly through his friendship, Kalra (a sworn bachelor and a promiscuous whoremonger) gets married and Ayesha, in fact, becomes a social worker in an NGO, working to reform the lives of prostitutes.

A curious scene occurs when, once again, the friends are drunk, and once again they are talking about sex and women, but this time they get into some heavy questions. 'When,' asks Sushil, 'is a woman at her loveliest?' Masterji ponders and replies, 'Just a few seconds after, in an act of consent and love, she has released her nectar.' Everyone is pleased with the answer and the next question follows, 'When is a woman at her ugliest?' Masterji changes 'ugliest' to 'most violent', and pronounces, 'Just a few seconds before she releases her nectar.' The descriptions of the friends in this scene are interesting. They are all eyes and ears; they are ready to get late for the wedding ('Rinku will get what he has to; we are here because of friendship') and they want to just keep drinking and talking.

A woman, even this very translator, could get envious of the close male bonding. In fact, I have always envied these male friendships that are prolific in Hindi films and literature.

Their dark side is as apparent in the novel as their good vibes. Ayesha wisely removes herself from the first floor and does not return, spending the whole night downstairs somewhere with the women. Sangita does not interact with her husband's male friends, even though they might call her *bhabhi*, or sister-in-law, and treat her with respect. Vandana commits suicide directly because of them. Her husband will not stay home even though she pleads and threatens suicide. He tells a lie and escapes. He stays at Sushil's party until midnight, then gets stuck and spends the night there. Vandana, tired of waiting, broken-hearted, frustrated and lonely, kills herself.

The friendships and the friends' circle persist, however, until the very end when Sangita and Masterji's baby is born and everyone hovers around. What are we to make of this extremely strong bond?

For Masterji, despite his friendship with Ayesha, and his love for her and various other women, the world is divided into men's and women's. Education, personality, work and fortitude does, of course, cross-cut the genders: both women and men are educated; both are strong and decisive; both work outside the home; and both suffer and fight for survival and peace of mind. But he talks about 'we friends' as against 'women in their friendships'. He muses on male bonding, and how men boast and spin yarns among themselves, not least about their sexual prowess. 'Do women do the same among themselves?'

he wonders. 'They talk very little about these things, just as men talk a lot,' he speculates.

Not only is the chief protagonist a man, and a sensitive, likeable man, he has half a dozen friends who are all to be understood as more or less good people. The women characters are more scattered and incompletely drawn, and seen always through the eyes of Masterji. He is open to them and does report their views, often in their own voices. We empathise with Amma, Sushil's mother, Vandana, Sangita, Mina, Pushpa, and most of all Ayesha. We toss around questions about them when Masterji does, especially about Ayesha, but also about Amma. Finally, however, we feel that there is more to them than has been revealed. Masterji continues to speculate about, and regard Vandana, Sangita and Ayesha as mysteries, and so do they come across to us.

Which brings us back to the male friends and the man. In Chapter 20 'Sangita says No', we have a sizeable discussion of the problem called patriarchy and male chauvinism, which has all been hinted at before but in passing.

Masterji worries that if he goes too far in his declaration of love to Sangita, and pleads too humbly with her, it will neither be good for him nor for her. Homes where men submit to women and women dominate over men are pits of conflict, he tells us. Then he worries: in thinking this, is he being a male chauvinist? What is wrong with women having power? Isn't that how America acts—unwilling to let weaker nations rise lest they assert equality with it? Does every powerful being, whether individual or state, want to hold back all those striving towards power? Is this why the whole world is, in fact, a pit of conflict?

The Crux of the Matter

To conflate patriarchy with the world order, and his probable male chauvinism with America's domination over developing nations, is a brilliant move. The novel is a dissertation on hierarchy. The hierarchy of gender is compared to the hierarchy of caste, in turn to that of class, of religion, of age and education—and in the strongest extension of the metaphor—to that of nations. In each case, the problem is that the weaker party, whether woman, or Dalit, or a poor, oppressed person, or an uneducated, backward person or nation, wishes to rise out of their mire of backwardness. They are not allowed to do so by those in power. Alliances shift, and those who are newly powerful practice the same politics of control on those struggling to rise.

That is why Jatavs and Brahmans are equated by assorted characters. It is presented as a demographic phenomenon, partly a historical and ideological one. But overall, through the prism of Masterji's consciousness, it is a problem that is philosophical and psychological: what is this proclivity of people and of groups to dominate and control? To oppose the downtrodden when they try to rise?

I chose to discuss the wedding days at length because they epitomise the characteristic of the novel that makes it what it is: a story of the everyday affairs of normal human beings who *happen to be* Dalits: their love affairs, marriages, family relationships, friendships, careers, scandals, decisions, weaknesses and glories.

This is perhaps an exemplar of the 'intellectual emancipation' that contemporary scholar and historian Anupama Rao talks about.

> Throughout the twentieth century, anticaste thinkers related struggles for caste equality with global movements for human emancipation. Indeed, it was through acts of political commensuration, that is, through explicit comparisons between caste and race, and later, between caste and class, that caste (and the evil of untouchability, in particular) came to be addressed as a historically determined form of quite general processes of inequality and subordination. (Rao p 128.)

What is 'Dalit'?

In their 1973 Dalit Panther Manifesto, the Dalit Panthers famously defined the meaning of Dalit: 'Who is a dalit? Members of scheduled castes and tribes, Neo-Buddhists, the working people, the landless and poor peasants, women and all those who are being exploited politically, economically, and in the name of religion' (in Murugkar 1991: 237).

Similarly, 'Dalit literature' has been equated with texts produced by writers with a 'Dalit consciousness' (Muktibodh 1992: 267). What, then, determines this Dalit consciousness? How do you develop it? Is it different from simply being Dalit, i.e., can non-Dalits have Dalit consciousness? Are there Dalits who do not have it, and why not? Finally, how do we judge the authenticity of it, either its experience or its expression?

Limbale goes so far as to suggest that the character of Dalit consciousness is univocal. He writes, 'The experiences narrated in Dalit literature are very similar. Untouchables' experiences of untouchability are identical' (2004: 35). This is what is precisely challenged by Navaria, who separates groups and classes within Dalits. He emphasises 'Worlds within Worlds'.

The key concept, as Brueck (353) points out, around which most Dalit authors and critics—Limbale, Valmiki, Naimishray—rally is the idea of 'Dalit consciousness'. There is a sense in their work of a singular 'consciousness' that for them underlies the emergence of Dalit literature. Further, it is a gauge to test the authenticity of any given work. 'The function of the theoretical concept of Dalit consciousness is articulated in the expressive and interpretive practices of writing and reading. Dalit consciousness has emerged in recent years in a large body of Dalit literary criticism as a theoretical tool with which the architects of Dalit literary culture are able to set boundaries for the growing genre of Dalit literature as well as launch a distinctly Dalit critique of celebrated works of Hindi literature' (Brueck 353).

In many ways, Navaria echoes mainstream Dalit consciousness. He shows Premchand in a dream sequence, and refers to him in other places in a critical vein, similar to other Dalit critics. He speaks repeatedly about Ambedkar as the beacon light for Dalits from whom they derive, or should derive, their primary energy. However, in the same dream sequence, he shows many sleeping homes who do not respond to a call to rise in the name of Ambedkar. His constant comparisons with gender and feminism, class conflict and Marxism, and global inequality and postcolonial thought, all serve to argue further the point about internal differentiation, and the utter and total lack of any unity of consciousness.

Navaria must have worried about this:

> ...arbiters of Dalit literature are constructing a critical framework based on the rhetorical practice of strategic essentialism. Dalit consciousness is the Dalit literary sphere's

> rendering of this practice for the political purpose of making an intervention into the mainstream literary-cultural sphere and claiming there a small space of their own in which they have the power to determine, by means of this essentialist concept, what authors and what texts may also share that space. (Brueck 355).

Brueck's invocation of Gayatri Spivak's 1985 piece on strategic essentialism is reminiscent of Marx's emphasis on the singularity of the working class, which many subsequent Marxists challenged. Similarly for feminists, there is always a negotiation between the politically expedient one-ness of women, and by implication, men, and the existential and artistic reality of plurality, easily recoverable in research (see Kumar 1994, 2001.)

The Insider-Outsider Dilemma

My own experience as a translator of this novel may contribute to the discussion of Dalit consciousness. If I am not a Dalit, should I feel diffident as a writer in translating and speaking for Dalit consciousness? I have never hesitated to write about the West (though from the East), about men (though a woman), about lower classes (though privileged), and about disabled or otherwise disadvantaged people while personally sharing none of their disadvantage. Partly, I have treated 'difference' metaphorically. Thus, for me, the 'wretched of the earth' are not only the materially or politically dispossessed, which I am not, but the otherwise victimised as well, such as those who suddenly, unaccountably, lose their beloved, as I did. *We*, all the hurt and abandoned who experience that loss, are the true and authentic 'wretched of the earth'.

Partly, I have achieved an intellectual self-confidence where I can justify speaking for the 'Other' precisely because no one is essentially fixed in 'one' identity or category, either 'the self' or 'the other'. Imagine my surprise, then, to discover myself responsible for a novel in which all the characters are Dalit and everyone is judged by their caste, and no *savarna* voice can speak for lower castes or Dalits.

Really?

But if I plead the case that mine is as authentic a voice as anyone's, am I saying that the author Ajay Navaria has not succeeded in depicting the existential suffering of Dalits but, once again, shown caste to be merely a discourse, a category, a weapon used differentially?

To some extent, yes. The author, just like the narrator-protagonist in the novel, is himself privileged. Not only is the narrator-protagonist educated, well-off and sophisticated in his consciousness, he is fair and good-looking. He has rich and successful friends. A Dalit is by definition downtrodden. Once you are not downtrodden, you are not a Dalit. It is analogous to my weeping of the woes of 'women' without acknowledging that, along with me, many women are, in fact, supremely privileged and powerful. And if the privileged insider can speak of their downtrodden communities, so can the intelligent, aware outsider who is not of the same blood lineage but shares the politics.

The author questions it all. One could wish that he would question yet more, or less, depending on one's perspective.

There is, however, another dimension of pain. 'I had not asked his caste,' he says. 'I had understood by now that people with my non-casteist thinking were in a tiny minority in our society.' There is this tiny group that one may belong to. One may then feel marginalized and misunderstood by the majoritarian groups. To have no voice is painful no matter where you stand.

Conclusion

The most important thinking point for me has been the ways in which the novel is both a rallying cry for emancipation and a story well told. I am satisfied to say that the immanence of caste in Navaria's novel provides its Dalit consciousness. We need to focus on an appreciation of its aesthetic content. The story of a young man with literary-philosophical interest, who goes through several love interests and groups of friends, who grows from a relatively little-rooted young lecturer to a mature professor and father in the course of the novel...there is a thickness to the plot no matter who he were. That he is Dalit is a central and essential identity of the man—the son, the brother, the thinker, the teacher, the social worker, the lover, the father. It would do unforgiveable injustice to the book to ignore the story of the man in favour of the story of the *Dalit* man. However, if we accept the analogy of low caste or Dalit with women, as the novel often presents, then one can *never* subsume the man's Dalit identity under some kind of a neutral middle-class one, much as we could not treat a female protagonist as some sort of a neutral 'person' ignoring her gendered identity, naturally enmeshed in gendered politics, at every turn.

If Dalit literature based on a notion of Dalit consciousness was one kind of a constructive response to the re-structuring of caste at the dawn of capitalist modernity, when caste could be theorised and imagined away, *Worlds within Worlds* provides an approach to caste mired in globalism and universalism. Its world is one of an everyday social inequality and tussle, accompanied by pain, where older hierarchies of caste are replaced by highly politicised sub-caste identities, both grosser and more fine-tuned than earlier divisions. Within these identities new battles have emerged, including alliances and cross alliances, conflicts that seem stark and unresolvable, often using the language of religion and always of class divisions. In this world, caste has been re-imagined as a tool to be wielded variously at every level. At the same time, within each sub-caste and expanded family, there is an ironic mirroring of the cultural practices of other sub-castes and families. The pain of the author-narrator lies both in the fact and in the *invisibility* of the fact to all.

The novel, through its ironic presentation of such a globalised world full of pain and struggle, is a re-definition of Dalit consciousness. It is an important and intriguing intervention in all the debates about Dalit literature and Dalit consciousness. Its universalism, its comparative consciousness, and its effortlessly drawn human and humane world deserves further interpretation, for which this Foreword is just the beginning.

Let us end with one of the most trivial but sweetest moments in the book. Women are singing their abusive songs at the *haldi* ritual and the grandmother, Amma, like many, feels that they go overboard.

> 'Don't get into these songs Ayesha,' said Amma. 'This is only for uneducated people, using songs to mouth abuses.'
>
> 'Well, well. Look at our Saviour, Lady Bridegroom's Mother.' Bari bua gave Amma a hug. 'My sweet old mother, her Ladyship, the Bridegroom's Mother.' Bua sang out the last part.

That is our culture, our history, our relationships, our politics. 'Our'? Yes, of *our* world—the nation, the world, the community, the family—that is, of worlds, and of *worlds* within *worlds*.

Nita Kumar

CHAPTER ONE

Meeting Ayesha

'Look at life only with the eyes of a small child, as if with the shock of discovery.'

I said it softly, waving a fly away with a hand. How did a fly come into this restaurant, airconditioned and luxurious as it was? I said it, but could not decide if she could even understand it.

I also wanted to say that in life every single instant was as important for a new start as a full life. Also, that the world did not consist of the 10 or 20 selfish, violent people because of whom she had reached where she was now. They were but a corner of the world, stony and sharp, and the opposite of them were the soft and attractive parts like her, her mother, or my own father. That's what made the world complete.

I knew that she would not understand all this. Maybe her lack of education was at fault. Her fifteen-year-old profession had set down roots in her brain which had sprouted their own tendrils. How, despite that, had she even kept alive her innocence; and more than that, her good humour? How had those not been scorched into cinders in the hot afternoon sun? Doubtless, the humour had wilted somewhat, but its life and warmth were far from dead.

'This is very important for you to know,' seeing her silent, I said after some time.

'Why?' The word fell out very softly from her lips.

There was no expression on her face as she said it. There was no curiosity in her brown eyes. She had no reaction to what I said…and no expectation of an answer to her question. The 'why' was just a word, not even disguised as a question. It was a useless word, and an unwanted word.

It was not, of course, a useless or undesirable word for me. It had come from a place where the horizons of the mind get blurry, where dark and light meet intimately.

Her brown, silky hair was open and fell over her cheeks. The shampooed hair would fall on her eyes and she would keep pushing it back behind her ears. Then the hair would softly slip and fall and she would tuck it back again. This was annoying me, though her face had nothing but winning innocence on it.

Was she actually so lovely and innocent or was that just my imagination?

The last few days had driven me to this question. Her uplifted nose seemed to boast a kind of pride, but in her chin, soft as risen bread, was the same innocence as in her eyes.

This happened last September, when we had first met. We had had long conversations on the phone but had not found the time to meet in person. Although she would be very keen to meet, but for me it was neither possible nor proper.

'How did you...' I paused, because I wanted to look into her eyes. She raised her eyes and looked questioningly at me, as I continued, '...begin to trust me?' I completed my question, trying to find the response in her eyes.

If she had listened with her eyes down, she could have hidden her feelings. I wanted to get the answer to my question not from her lips, but her eyes.

'I don't know' was all she could say, finding me staring. She kept running her fingers around the edges of the round glass table. 'I liked you...from the instant I saw you.' She stopped. 'You seem very innocent.' She was still playing with the table. She raised her eyes, then lowered them. Her eyes were bright.

'Are you in love with me?' I whispered. There was an anxiety in the whisper.

I was worried at repeating these words from the past. I had got over the worry with deliberate smiles and force of will. But it had spilled over into my question. Long ago, my wife Vanjha had said these words to me. 'And you?' she asked, her brown eyes on me.

I had not expected her to turn the question around to me. I was silent. Not that the answer to the question was difficult for me, but it was her answer I wanted. I had many questions, and the answers to all of them were with someone like her. Then the 'someone like her' kept echoing in my ears. It was silenced after a long time.

'Love is blind,' seeing me silent, she said after some time.

'Perhaps love is multiply disabled…perhaps love is full of insecurities and very stubborn because of its many disabilities,' I said all this, but I was studying her face. She seemed to understand, but also not understand. She looked at me with her long-lashed brown eyes like a small, lovely child.

They were the first tingling days of spring. The air was losing its chill. The water kept at night, however, was still cold in the morning. Not so cold that you didn't want to touch it, as it had been the month before. I had left home after a bath with water warmed up by the geyser.

Those days of spring were days of uncontrollable energy and leaping desire.

It was the middle of the day. The time for 'Happy Hours' in Big Banana. 'Happy Hours' meant a free beer on the purchase of a beer. She had already known this, and had explained it to me. I knew she would not let me pay the bill today either. She always insisted on paying our bills.

'This is for my pleasure. I want to pay for it,' she would insist. Although I did not have the means to pay those big bills, I would always argue out of politeness.

'What will you take?' she changed the subject. Her eyes were still on the glass table.

'Anything…whatever you like.' I could not take my eyes off her magical face with its wind-blown hair.

'Whiskey?' she smiled. Her eyes were teasing.

'As long as no one thinks we are alcoholics.' I made her laugh by silently miming a drunkard's behaviour.

'Let people go to hell,' she shrugged. 'Let's have beer.' She gestured to the waiter who was standing some distance away, looking at us, waiting for our summons. He was perfectly trained, alert but silent.

'Get some lager beer for me,' I said. She heard me but said nothing.

'One strong and one lager beer…and some finger chips… some nuts.' She did not look at the waiter once. She said all this so easily in English, it was difficult to believe that she was only a class X graduate from a public high school. Apart from at these times, she always spoke in Hindi.

I had tried a few times to have long conversations with her in English but she had made it clear that she did not know more English than this.

'Anything else, ma'am?' the waiter asked, bending low.

She shook her head to say no. He retreated.

Watching him, I thought that, apart from his work, he too must always speak in Hindi. To appear high-class we were all speaking in English and wanted to be seen speaking in English. How was this different to when a Brahmin does his performance and is accepted as the highest in society?

'He must be from Himachal.' I had thought on seeing the waiter's sharp nose.

'It's not called "ledger", it's called "lager",' she corrected me softly after the waiter had moved away.

My first thought was of Nirmal Verma's stories' use of 'lager'. My second thought was that it's a difference at another level as well. In our neighbourhood we all said 'ledger' when all the time it was actually 'lager'.

So, who would be able to survive this gap between the people and the gentry? Will 'lager' stay 'lager' or will it devolve to 'ledger', just as 'lantern' became 'lalten'? Will the word prove more powerful and decide its meaning or will the popularity and domestication of the meaning decide the word?

She had become silent after correcting me. There was no sarcasm in what she said. Nor had I felt embarrassed. It seemed to me that if I had said the wrong word to the waiter, he would have understood as well and brought me 'lager beer.' Of course, he would also have grasped my economic level.

English! English has the place today exactly as the Brahmins' Sanskrit had 1,500 years ago—a time mysteriously called a Golden Age…research on which still awaits.

It was an exhausting, and even more, a painful, evening when I had first met her.

A complete neighbourhood of Dalits had been reduced to ashes in the small *qasba* of Gohana in Haryana. We rushed there as soon as we heard. The fire had been set to our own houses.

Dibang was talking to a politician on NDTV who, even on TV, was expressing his caste prejudice.

The neigbourhood was deserted, and burning away with loud noises and crackles. There were pigs, dogs and hens in the place. They had all collected on one side.

We were helpless and like cowards watched our life's savings go up in flames. Many girls were about to get married but their wedding trousseaus had turned to ashes; the girls were not there. The administration had no idea where the thousands of people living here for hundreds of years had vanished.

When I reached home the next afternoon and fell asleep, I awoke only in the evening. The tiredness and pain had not worn off. Kalra called. In spite of many refusals he kept insisting I come over and finally, I had to go. I thought of it as a distraction. I did not guess what kind of a distraction it would be.

I met her there. My first meeting. I was sitting in the drawing room with Kalra. He had handed me a drink but I just sat there holding it, paralysed. That's when she came out from an inside room.

'Where is Rana?' Kalra had asked her. Asked her in a special way. He was smiling as he looked at her—a smile full of secrets.

'Lying inside…finished.' She had made the sign of a zero with her thumb and forefinger. 'But really, he is a devil.' She laughed. She stretched out, picked up a glass and downed it in one gulp.

I looked at her, shocked.

'Go, call Rana here,' Kalra said, looking at me.

I went inside. Rana smiled as he saw me.

'When did you come?' His voice was exhausted.

'I just got back from Gohana. You must have heard.'

'Yes, I heard…it's a tragedy.' He continued to lie there, spent. 'As long as they are poor, they will continue to be killed.'

'No, they were not poor. For their community, they were well off. Come on, Kalra is calling.'

I had wanted to ask him about what had been going on in that room, but was unable to. He got up, and, tying on his *tahmad*, emerged. He sat down on the chair opposite her. She was chewing something quietly. She did not look up at him. I studied her closely. There could be no doubt any longer about what she was. She looked about twenty-five or twenty-six; later she had announced herself to be thirty.

'This is Ayesha…my friend,' Kalra said, looking at me.

Kalra always spoke about girls like her with respect, whereas Rana always referred to them as 'whore' or 'bitch'.

'Ayesha, this is my friend, a university professor.' Kalra looked at her, and then at me. 'Professor, she has a problem that only you can solve.'

I said 'Hello' to her but, contrary to my expectations, she did not respond. She merely raised her hand and waved her fingers.

'What can I do for you?' When I said this, she raised her face and probed me with her brown eyes. Looking at the innocence of her face, I tried to re-think. Were my ideas about her nonsense—was she an innocent creature? She could not be…could she really be…?

'Ayesha, don't bother us here. Go inside and talk.' Kalra's words made her get up without a word and start for the inside room.

I looked at Kalra questioningly as if to say 'Why not here' but Kalra nodded in the direction of the room and signalled with his eyes to say 'Go and find out.' I could not refuse him. He had done me many favours. A debtor does not argue.

I reached inside. She was sitting on the bed. I pulled up a chair to the bed and sat down. She arose and bolted the door. She was standing directly in front of me.

I realised that I had been right the first time. Her innocence was a ploy. She suddenly came forward and put her arms around my neck. To my surprise, I had no reaction. Maybe because those were the moments of guilt.

'What is all this?' I came to my senses as if a 1000-watt bulb had been turned on in the darkness.

'A gift for you from your friend.' She did not seem to mind my flinging off her arms. Her face showed no complaint.

'No…no…please…behave yourself…tell me what you had to say.' I reached the door as I spoke and, unbolting it, opened it wide.

I looked back at her. She stared at me with wide, unblinking eyes. I must have panicked. It was my first brush with a sex worker. Seeing her silent, I left the room. Kalra laughed loudly to see me return. Rana too.

'I knew it, Professor…you will not be able to share anyone's pain and sorrow.' Kalra gave me a hearty smack on the back and went into the room. I heard the door close behind me.

'Go, Professor, she is calling you.' Kalra returned after a few minutes. Meanwhile, I had played with thoughts of running away but had not budged. Why, after all?

'Go and listen.' Kalra was not ordering me, but persuading me affectionately.

'Call her here.' I waved my hands to say no.

'She is not going to force herself on you. She is a woman, not a man. You should listen to your close friends. Go on, she won't be pushy, I've told her.' He came forward and put his arm around my shoulders. 'You are an upright man, Professor. People like me need faith to live, and people like you demonstrate that faith.'

Kalra's eyes had both respect and a complaint.

Listening to all this, I was in a quandary.

Is this why they say that God likes his faithful and simple devotees best? Is this why in the Gita Krishna advises his devotees to keep their eyes closed? Is God too, like Kalra, once clever, now disillusioned with the world, simply busy reassuring his simple devotees? If he is in fact like that, then why is he so passive? How can a passive, or dead, person be the support of a live, able man?

Kalra never struck me as bad. He had looked after his younger brothers and sisters after his parents' death. Because of his responsibilities he had never married.

I got up and went inside. Upon seeing me she stood up. As I sat down on the chair she went and bolted the door again. I looked at her questioningly.

'Don't be afraid, Masterji.' I liked her calling me 'Masterji'. Her voice held respect.

She came and sat on the armrest of my chair. I looked at her as if to say, 'See, there you go again.' She understood. 'Okay, okay,' she said, and quickly sat on the bed instead.

'Why did you call me?' I asked her after looking at her for some time. I felt awkward.

'I wanted to talk to you.' She seemed to understand my awkwardness and impatience. Her eyes were full of fun. At the same time, she did not look as if she was scheming…it was the fun of an innocent child.

'Your name?' she asked with playfulness.

'How does it matter? I am not planning to meet you again.' I said rudely, feeling I was being teased.

'Still…' She did not seem to mind my rudeness.

'Siddharth.' I deliberately told her a made-up name.

'Your name suits you, Mr Yogi.' She laughed with the same playfulness.

'And yours?' I asked despite myself. Maybe there was a human curiosity in me regarding her. Or did I want to talk to her as well…surely, but only talk. To get to know a new and unfamiliar world. After all, she was also a part of human society…and so on.

'Ayesha.' She puckered her lips.

'Are you?' I wanted to ask if she was a Muslim, but kept quiet. It would have been the same lack of courtesy to ask that as to ask about someone's caste. If she is a Hindu, how does it matter; and if she is not, does it matter?

She is what she is, and her being her is nothing more than one single circumstance. Maybe a statistic, or a statistical event…such as is needed by the government for its census or political parties to incite riots occasionally. She herself would need it, apart from birth and marriage, only when she is herself no more.

'Go ahead and ask, Masterji.' She asked neutrally upon my being silent for so long.

'No, it's nothing.'

'I am not a Muslim…That's what you wanted to ask, wasn't it?' She said in the same neutral way. Maybe her lack of emotion had become a part of her nature. She could say anything very simply.

'No…no…nothing like that…Your name is such.' I was embarrassed.

'This was the name my mother liked,' she said, raising her eyes to mine. 'Then I saw that it brought me some professional benefits. Would you like to know what?'

'What?' I asked without thinking.

'Hindu clients like Muslim women. They feel satisfied. They claim that Muslim women are hot. It was by chance that when I mentioned my name Ayesha in front of a client, he immediately joined Khanum to it, and asked, "Muslim?" and, Masterji, I jokingly said "Yes". That made him crazy. He was a weakling, but upon hearing this, he became a rabid Pathan. "Don't leave this work. If you ever need money, call me" he said, and gave me extra and gave me his card.'

'Who was he?' I tried to curb my curiosity but had to ask.

'I don't remember now, some businessman. But I had found a good strategy. Once, in the start, I found someone from my caste. He was sad to see me in this profession.

He wanted to get me a job in an NGO but I refused. He would have used our common caste to enjoy me privately and hand me a salary of 5,000 or 6,000 a month. The bastard Mr Virtuous Social Service Man…if I were to go to him in my old age, he wouldn't give me the time of day.' The amazing thing was that there was no bitterness in her voice.

I was speechless on hearing her experiences. Not that these things were new for me. I had seen the mutual lack of trust between Hindus and Muslims while doing my post-graduation from Maulana Safdar Ali Muslim University. This mutual lack of trust, and even contempt on both sides, was born by women…and the poorest men. Firoz and I discussed this all the time. He was among my best friends. He loved Nigar passionately, and she him.

'She is a Qureshi. Her family will never let her marry me,' he had told me when I'd ask him about marrying Nigar. 'They will let her marry you,' he'd say, laughing a feeble laugh.

'Meaning?' I asked.

'Meaning that you are both butchers.' I laughed to hear him refer to my caste in this way. 'You and Nigar are truly butchers. Even in love you are determined.'

This is what he was upset about. He knew about my relationship with Vandana. Vandana in those days was committed to a friendship with me.

'Is this really your name?' I had meanwhile made myself normal again. 'Usually, they make up a name.'

'Oh, so you have a lot of experience…and what about your name?' Her sarcasm matched mine.

'What do I have to fear?'

'And you think I am afraid? All the police of this police station say namaste to me. I go around in the car of the Deputy Superintendent of Police.' Her head was high and her eyes gleamed with pride.

'Are you married?' I could not guess what she wanted with that question.

'No' escaped me. Why would I tell her about Vandana's death? I had not yet married Sangita. How best to describe myself—married, bachelor or widower? I found it easiest to hide. Then I thought, wouldn't Kalra have told her about my private life?

'I want to do something for you, Masterji.' Her intimate 'Masterji' won me over again.

'I…would…only with my wife…' I mumbled something incoherently.

'You are insulting me.' She had stood up. Her voice had force, rather than hope.

In a flash, she had unbelted her maroon gown and slipped it down her shoulders. It slithered to the ground. She was wearing nothing underneath except for a belt of black metal that was around her well-formed narrow waist. This was a sweet moment, a moment of drunkenness, of guilt. In that one instant, a dozing human recklessness raised its cobra-like hood.

'They are all the same.' The thought brought me to my senses.

'I am the one, Ayesha, who is not insulting you.' I picked up the gown, put it on her shoulders and tied it at her middle. 'This is not about the body, but about the soul. About honour. How can someone buy you with a few silver coins?'

That was an intense moment, emotional and unexpected.

She stood silently, like a statue made of metal. I, too, stood for some time, then sat down, then stood, then looked at her and sat down again. What am I doing? I wondered.

'Do you want to say something?' I asked. But she stood completely silent. She was not there. Her veil had got stuck somewhere, perhaps on a thorn in a bush from the past.

I stood up. She raised her eyes to me but was still silent, not there. I opened the door and went out.

That must have been her final weapon, and it had gone waste. She had nothing else she could use. All this was on the outer limits of her experiences and expectations.

'Masterji, I am leaving with a grudge in my heart.' She had got dressed and was leaving. She said this to me unwatched by anyone.

Rana had sat at the steering of his new Maruti Esteem. Kalra and I stood at the door. 'He has a new car,' Kalra had told me. It was white. Rana was mad about the colour white. I knew him for about two or two-and-a-half years, and had never seen him wear anything but white.

Rana was a strong, hard-working man. His village was in western Uttar Pradesh. He had left behind terrible poverty and reached somewhere. He had educated himself and become an officer in an important government firm. He was a capable and strong officer.

All those strata that had so far been banned from the professions of engineer, doctor and professor now had people in these professions after Independence, thanks to the Reservation policy. These people are ordinary people of the country, and look like ordinary people. With their entry into government professions, the ordinary person has a different view of high-caste people. Millions of the underdogs of the nation now believe that they can also become doctors and engineers. Reservations have empowered the nation by making democracy popular and accessible.

Kalra both took some favours from Rana and gave some. Slowly, this interdependence had turned into a strange friendship.

'Rana, this professor is a "Triple P" type of person.' Kalra put his arm around me. Rana gave a loud laugh. Ayesha smiled to herself. Her smile was provoked, annoyed.

As the car left the house, Ayesha shook hands with me and I felt a chit of paper in my hands. I kept it in my pocket away from everyone's eyes. It had her mobile number.

'What is this "Triple P", Kalra?' I asked as soon as the car left.

'Triple P means "Permanent, Paid, Prostitute"...Wives. What are wives but a permanent and single-focused prostitute?' Kalra lit a cigarette.

Kalra's face was expressionless. His face had no scorn or contempt in making such a big statement. His thinking about women had a malodorous quality to it. Would he include his mother in this category? I was unable to ask him, much as I wanted to.

'We are the T.P.P. types,' he said after some time when I said nothing. 'Temporary Paid Prostitutes. Why should we keep this fungus in our homes? Whenever you are ready, spill some money in the market, and she will come like a Lakshmi to your house. Treat her as you like and stretch out to sleep,' he added, taking a deep drag.

'She won't eat up your ears twenty-hours a day like a Permanent. The work is the same in both cases, but the second wants rights as well. They will use the excuse of children, as if the pleasure had been any the less for them. This Rana... my two brothers...every bastard is a victim of his wife. These women...these women know Chinese torture...killing atom by atom...can you understand how tragic that is?' he had almost started shouting.

This male chauvinist perspective of Kalra's usually emerged after a few drinks. On an everyday basis, he was civil and courteous towards women. I had even seen him come to blows with a man who had tried to make advances towards a woman.

'All women are not the same, just as all men are not the same,' I was finally forced to say.

'No, all women are the same...whores, bitches, daughters of bitches.' He had downed one too many. He descended to abuse.

'Our mothers as well?'

These were pin-points of words. He was pricked and bled. His tired eyes were red.

'With their men, yes,' he said in an undertone.

This was his violent side. He glared at me like a tiger. His eyes were thick and bloodshot. I understood that he was talking, not about men and women, but about male and female, which—in his drunken state—he was converting to the roles of husband and wife.

Was it not after entering the married state that male and female got transformed to men and women?

Kalra was unable to understand the play of these two opposite forces. Perhaps he would be unable to accept that marriage was the conditional event for these two forces. He had understood only the power of money and had presumed that that was the foundation of everything else.

Kalra may have been wrong or right in holding his perspective, but in our intellectual democracy, he was surely equal and free.

'Women probably think the same about men.' He kept quiet. For some time, we were both quiet.

'I should be going,' I said and stood up. Kalra said nothing.

Why was I unable to touch Ayesha…I kept thinking all the way. Perhaps I find sex workers repulsive because they have relationships with so many men, I answered myself. Then why did I not find Madhurima repulsive? Before my marriage I had a relationship with Madhurima, and she was not only married but 10 years my senior. Had she not had relationships with other men before me? Maybe that was fine because she was not a professional. But does that make a difference? Was hers not a bigger crime? And, like Madhurima, had I not reached Vandana and Sangita a soiled leftover? Do we indeed become soiled leftovers? Could I not move ahead with Ayesha only because I did not know her at all? After all, we are not animals. Was my thinking clouded over by ideas of purity? Sex was simply difficult for me without some attraction. I was like a helpless insect trapped in a web of questions.

The questions stayed with me all night.

CHAPTER TWO

Ayesha's Story

'This is not the time for beer, by the way.' As Ayesha spoke, I was freed of this burden of memories of our first meeting. She had realised I was elsewhere, and had been watching me silently.

'I have no idea about all this…and when you don't know, you can be off the mark in your choice. I am just with you. Very seldom do I drink both beer and whiskey.'

'Why didn't you tell me…I thought you wanted it. I don't at all.'

'I thought you did…that's why I agreed.'

'Is this not love? We are ready to do what we imagine the other wants, without complaint,' she said, looking into my eyes.

'It could also simply be respect for each other.' I did not want her to be under any illusion about me. Sangita had left me the month before. But we were still husband and wife, and not divorced.

'Then what is love?' It was not an eager question.

'Maybe coffee would be better?' I changed the subject.

'Yes, certainly, coffee and love have a lot in common. A satisfying and strange sweetness. Is it not?' she said, searching for something in my eyes. Maybe the faith that loneliness was not inevitable. She had already declared that she would never steal my wife's rights. And anyway, how was that possible?

'That, I don't know.' I was quiet. I wanted to say that it was not coffee and love but coffee and domesticity that had much in common…a kind of sweetness that was laden with a tongue-biting tang.

'What did you say?' she asked.

'Nothing…' I answered quickly. Can she read my thoughts? Bengalis can't be trusted after all.

Her eyes widened, then narrowed. She raised her hand slightly and the waiter appeared immediately. She ordered the waiter to cancel the previous order and to bring coffee.

The waiter took the order with lowered head and departed.

The waiter permitted no trace of complaint or annoyance to appear on his face. He was a waiter who understood the value of the customer in this time of globalisation and competition. Or was he aware of his status within the company's 'hire and fire' formula? Or with the harsh gaze of the floor manager behind him, in turn managed by the invisible eyes of the restaurant owner?

Ayesha had spoken to the waiter in English, and the waiter had also said 'Anything else?' after his 'Yes ma'am'.

'A woman should not be so weak as to follow this profession to fill her belly,' I found myself saying.

Why did I say it? Was I envious of her glamour? Did I want to bring her down by saying it? I thought she would mind it, but on the contrary, she smiled. I felt bad at her shamelessness.

'What do you think?' She paused an instant, then smiled. 'That this was my choice?' It was a question but with no resentment on her countenance.

'So, what do you teach, Masterji?' She changed the subject.

'Law…' I lied again. I had done Law by correspondence, but it was not my subject.

'That's why you're like this!' she said softly.

'Like how?' I laughed.

'Deceitful!' she laughed as well. 'Hindi teachers are nice… they are full of humanity,' she teased me. 'Just like my Arun sir.'

When she pronounced 'Arun sir' there was a special sweetness in her voice. Probably Arun sir had left a mark on her in her early years.

'Who was he?' I asked, but she had wandered off onto another path.

'The owner of the farm house we lived in threw my mother and me out one day. Ma had some disease. My father had left us when I was two or three years old.' She had paused, perhaps to take control of the flood within her. 'My father had suspicions about my mother...he considered me the owner's offspring. My mother told me, a few months before she died.' She stopped. The waiter appeared, put the coffee down and departed.

'Father was not wrong, but my mother was not wrong either.' She cleared her throat. 'What was wrong was that we were poor, we were slaves. After my mother died, I went to the farmhouse to meet the owner who my father suspected. The owner was not at home but I met his wife and daughter. My father had been correct. The daughter was a mirror image of me.' She took a sip of her coffee. 'Nice taste...' She nodded and raised her eyebrows in praise of the coffee. I followed her example, took a sip and echoed that the coffee was indeed good.

'My father was not wrong,' She continued, perhaps upon reading the curiosity in my eyes. 'Why would he raise his master's child? Even a stepmother wants that if she is kind enough to bring up another's child, the child be not her husband's bastard. But my mother was not wrong because all this had happened against her wishes. She was weak and she was desperate. The master had threatened to embroil my father in a false case and she gave in. She wanted to save her husband, and the same husband kicked her away.' She started needlessly blowing on her coffee. Maybe she was cooling down the embers in her soul.

'I can't call my real father "father", and I have no rights on the one I called father. Is there a law, Mr Lawyer, which can give me my father?' she laughed sarcastically…a sad laugh.

For an instant I felt as if all this was a fabrication. Every prostitute has such a story and every customer wants to hear such a story. Maybe the story helps in emotional blackmailing… but what did I have that she needed? And her unaffectedness in seeming unaffected also removed that thought. I felt as if she would burst into tears at any moment.

'And your work?' I asked.

'I became a receptionist in an office, and there it…began.' She spoke after some time and emphasizing 'began', kept silent. It was pointless to ask any more.

'Then I thought, if for a 1,000 or 1,500 a month this is what I have to do, then why not do it in style. Business is business. There is a market, and style is everything. Choice is a big thing. Then my English made my style stand out. I had such young and handsome suitors as one could only have dreamt of.' Her voice held desire.

'You should have left this work, Ayesha.'

'How? There are hundreds of calls from every side. Which ones to disregard? Hunger is a terrible thing. Starvation makes you forget all your self-respect. I have to be grateful to men for my work.' Her voice was full of contempt.

'Men also starve, but they don't do all this, they labour.' I had sympathy for her pain but I was deliberately provoking her.

'Masterji, you are a good man, but you don't know the world of men. Petty violence…smuggling…illicit middlemanship is the world of men, and how many have you seen in my profession, after all?' Her voice was full of pain. 'We are all equally products…or on the brink of becoming…'

I was indeed silenced by this. I thought of the report of growing male prostitution in the city. Maybe those who thought of humanity as a backward trait were promoting this cosmopolitan business in this cosmopolitan city. There were no men and women in this business, only two products, and at the most, males and females. These products had a market value that rose and fell in the share market like the Sensex. Colour, beauty, size, form and ability were key to their value, as was the English language.

This new market had bloomed into exotic gardens in the metropolises. The blooms may not have a smell, but they had magical colours.

'Masterji, women may be different in the beginning, but are all the same in the end.' She paused. 'But a man…is different from the beginning to the end. And women are less adulterous compared to men. Don't mind my saying this, but no matter how much love you give a man, he will not hesitate to turn around to taste another delicacy.'

This was a complex, not a simple, statement. I thought of Kalra. Ayesha did not trust men and Kalra did not trust women. I also thought of the 'gigolos' that Ayesha had talked about, who ruin themselves for women.

'All men?' I asked, but she did not answer.

'Mandarin Fort is my favourite hunting ground.' She changed the subject. 'Have you ever gone there?'

I shook my head.

Mandarin Fort was walking distance from the university. I had looked at it often in passing. In the daytime, it was totally deserted. As evening drew on, its mysteries deepened. The large cars of this large city meandered around like colourful cockroaches. In these large cars, underage children blew their horns in various meaningless ways. People thought of them as 'young', and the administration gave them driving licenses while thinking they were young. They could not give a damn what the administration thought of them. They drove, and they drove recklessly. They braked with a sharp screech if someone appeared in front of them. Their cars were often stuck in jams, then turned around swiftly. At none of this did they show fear or worry. On the contrary, they laughed loudly and slapped their companion's hands with their own to laugh some more. They looked at the faces of the poor who survived their cars with distaste as if they were dirty insects and spiders.

They were courageous children, but they were panic-stricken by their insecurity and their loneliness. They looked bloated with this fear. These evenings were the one source of happiness in their silent, deserted lives. Even though they lived in the same city, they did not see their parents for days on end. These children were sick, but their parents had no time for their cure.

Unlike middle-class parents, these parents were not earning for their children's 'future'. These children had not received what they wanted. While searching, they had either precociously become too old too early, or had said farewell to life by shooting or doping themselves to death. These were lonely, enfeebled, needy, high-caste children.

I worried: would the children of Dalits, too, become like this in some future generation?

CHAPTER THREE

Ayesha's Prejudices

'That place has its own charm,' Ayesha said, putting her hand over mine, and I came back as if from a long and horrible journey. 'That place has a fried fish with tartar sauce and a Bloody Mary that is unmatched. This place has them too, but neither the taste nor the atmosphere.'

'What kind of a person is Kalra?' I interrupted her. I was curious to know what Ayesha, full of contempt for men, thought of Kalra, whose opinion of women was extremely derogatory.

'Kalra is not bad at heart…but like me, he does not trust anyone…he is empty and insecure.' She sipped her coffee that had long got cold.

'Maybe he does trust you, and wants to fill up his emptiness with that.'

Her eyes were liquid. They were intimate, with an assurance that could give breath to life. The eyes were also shining with a question which was easy for me to understand but impossible to answer.

'That Rana, however, he is a devil, the bastard.' She smiled and winked, and in that wink, transformed into another Ayesha.

'Why?' I stared at her in surprise.

'That bastard has…' She showed a size with her fingers and smiled. 'This is how these Doms are.'

I was at a loss. I could not decide if she was praising us or bad-mouthing us, whether to be pleased or not.

'Is Rana a Dom?'

'Of course…scheduled castes are Doms, aren't they,' she said simply and sipped her coffee.

I knew that Rana was not a Dom. He was a Dhanuk by caste and always called himself higher than Valmikis. I was silent. I saw that the same fly had reappeared, and was buzzing near the coffee. Ayesha had waved it away from her cup, but the fly had come and sat there again. Kalra had also told me about this special thing about Rana. Ayesha waved the fly away again. It came and sat on my side.

I felt strange that this fly had entered this glamorous, air-conditioned restaurant.

'Maybe that's what women like?' I pressed on.

'Maybe…but if so, then why did Rana's wife leave him for someone else?' She looked at me while speaking, at my mouth open with surprise.

'You wouldn't know this but he used to cry when with me…a woman is not just a body. Right, Masterji? Everyone is hungry, but for love and caresses as well.' She waved away the fly yet again. Her cup still had coffee in it.

'A woman wants care on top of love. When a woman can become a mother and nurture the man, why can't a man become a father and nurture her? A husband should know how to be a friend and a father too, Masterji. A man does not become any less of a man by giving attention to a woman as if she were a child. Rana keeps crying now.'

'Do you not like Rana?'

'At first it was fine…as Kalra's friend. But not now…' She paused. 'These Doms are very dirty.'

'How do you know?' I stoked my anger by throwing water on the embers.

'I've seen their homes in the village…Just as you did not let the beggar touch you near the flyover, that's how they are, filthy and smelly.' She waved the fly away. 'You can see the fly but you can't swallow it, can you, Masterji?'

I thought of my village, where my own community lived in a dirty way. Most of them were poor, hard-working people. The one or two families that were well-off lived with pomp. What Ayesha was ascribing to caste was actually just about money.

'We are a high caste, Masterji.' She showed me the conch-shell and red bangles on her wrist. She touched her gold bangle. It may have been gold or just brass. I could not keep my attention off the fly that continued to hover around us.

'We are Raychaudhuris. Ayesha Raychaudhuri.' Her voice had pride.

I was nauseated to see this traditional pride on Ayesha's face. I felt like shouting at her, 'You bitch, you cheap prostitute. Here is another Dom standing in front of you for whom you are ready to swear devotion.' I was ashamed of myself.

'When did you get married?' I asked instead.

'How did you know?' she asked wide-eyed.

'These conch-shell and red bangles,' I signalled with my eyes.

'Oh, so you know that these are worn only by Bengali married women. I did marry, thinking I'd have a family, but that pig came only to live off my earnings.' She kept quiet, trying to control her feelings. She had become crude again when mouthing 'pig'. I watched her silently.

This was my style. I made the other fight with themselves and regain control. Everyone should have the strength to challenge and respond to themselves. She was learning this too, in the first few days of our friendship.

'I left him…I kicked him away,' she murmured after some time. She was in pain but also recovering from it.

'Who was he?'

'Someone from our own caste.'

I had not asked his caste. I had understood by now that people with my non-casteist thinking were in a tiny minority in our society.

Even if you refuse and turn away from it, your caste becomes your identity. My caste will not leave me till I die, and surely after that as well. This caste identity grasping me by the throat will not leave future generations either. From humans to gods, all are caste-bound. No change has taken place. Just that some gods increase or decrease in various castes. Then why do I want to run away from caste? Will we ever be able to end caste? Or am I building castles in the air?

'What caste are you, Masterji?' This was a new, and totally vernacular voice.

The fly balancing on the edge had fallen into the cup. 'Look at that,' she smiled at me pointing at it.

I wanted to tell her that I was not about to turn back from the direction in which I had already travelled. I also wanted to tell her that if Rana was a Dom, so were we all, Doms.

'Look at life like a small child, full of wonder,' was all I said.

She left. I told her the same thing again as she was leaving.

'I will.' She took my hand in both of hers as she left. 'Give some thought to me,' she said timidly. 'I don't want anything from you…just to keep a little space for you in my life.'

'You are my good friend,' were my last words to her that evening. Then we dragged ourselves back to our respective homes.

CHAPTER FOUR

Vandana, Through Thick and Thin

The morning was warm and bright. I had fallen asleep thinking. I was learning to love my new solitude again in this three-roomed university flat. I had got used to loneliness after Vandana's death, but Sangita had interrupted that and filled my emptiness with her affection.

The last 10 years had been an amazing mixture of the burdens and pleasures of love. Is everyone's life like that? Or was it just my life in which every moment was a bundle of unpredicted events?

Kalra, Rana, Vandana, Sangita—don't they all, in fact, simply tolerate events as they unfold? All of us, involuntarily, find events looming in front of us. They are happy events or tragic ones, exciting ones, terrifying ones…and powerless, we accept them with lowered eyelids but wide-open eyes…just silently accept them. At the most, depending on our energy, what we manage is to thrash out, trying to stop these events from happening, or once they have happened, to find a way out—dancing with joy if they were good events and singing our mourning songs if they were bad ones.

This is what everyone calls…life?

'Awake?' Amma had come and stood next to me. I had not heard a sound.

'Will you have tea?' She knew my habits.

'Yes, Amma.' My father called my grandmother 'Amma'. We brothers learnt the name from our uncles and adopted it. It was our mothers who were called 'Amma' or 'mai' in the neighbourhoods in which I had grown up.

'Sangita called,' Amma said. I looked at her with surprise. I did not understand if Amma was asking me or telling me about Sangita's call.

'She was asking about my health,' she answered my unspoken question.

Amma had a respiratory problem. A dust storm made her trouble worse. She kept much better in the green university campus compared to the pollution of the city. That is why, after our marriage, Sangita had insisted on bringing Amma here. Amma and Sangita had a deep friendship, not a mother-in-law–daughter-in-law relationship at all.

Although they knew each other a mere seven or eight months, it was as if they'd known each other for ages. When dada, my grandfather, died, Amma was just over 30. My father was 12 or 13 then. After him, there were two uncles and two aunts. Amma was given dada's job after his death. The department gave her a 'water carrier's' job. Amma, my darling Amma, must have borne such hardships—but she never talked about them.

'She wanted to meet me. She was saying "Amma, I am longing to see you."' Amma's voice was itself full of longing.

Does an old heart keep young nourished by this love and longing?

'Do I stop you?' I turned my face away.

'That's what I told her.' She sighed. 'I told her to come but she refused.'

'I am never around in the day. If she wants to meet you, let her do so,' I said, looking out of the window.

'She won't come here...I know her...she has been hurt... she was asking me to meet her somewhere outside.' Amma paused. 'You won't mind, will you?'

'Then go...she is your daughter-in-law...We are not legally divorced yet.' My voice had an unanticipated tone of hurt pride.

Amma looked crestfallen at this. She kept thinking, her eyes unblinking. I knew that she must be comparing her own unfortunate life with mine. She could not break relations with Sangita...and I was part of her blood and bones. She was in a strange conflict.

'Sangita is not like Vandana...I know Sangita. I may not have lived with Vandana, but I have experience of life...

that girl wanted others to live by her principles, but did not believe in any herself. She wanted the whole world to kill itself, if needed, for her happiness...what is the point of such selfishness if it leaves you totally alone? Sangita is just the opposite, she wants to grow along with everyone.' Amma took a deep breath and stopped.

Amma was so logical that she could take the most complicated thing and explain it simply. Father had this quality too; he must have got it from Amma. I had inherited dadaji's temper; that's what Amma always told me. She still loved to talk about dadaji; she did not re-marry after dadaji. My mother told me that Amma was beautiful in her time. If she wanted, she could have re-married, because in our caste women re-marry as many times as they like.

Why she had not re-married was something she explained to Sangita one day when Sangita asked.

'I did not feel like belonging to someone else after him. He had given me more love and affection than needed for one lifetime. He had a temper, but he had as much love. Then, I had started earning, so I did not need to depend on anyone.' Sangita had told me all this.

My Amma, my aged Amma, steadied herself with hands on knees and went off. She came back with tea. 'Try to talk once, won't you,' she said as she left. I had understood Amma's philosophy of life. She accepted events, good or bad, as a rule of nature. She accepted every turn in life. I had never heard her complain. She believed in moving ahead after every turn, and in fighting and searching for new paths to happiness.

Vandana had never listened to Amma. She did not like to call her home. She did not like my 'illiterate' mother, and my father was 'casteist' by her definition. We had to move out just six months after our marriage. She insisted on our taking a new place near the college where I taught. Vandana was friends with Nigar; and then through Firoz, she and I came closer and closer.

The past spread itself like ragged sheets in front of me.

I had passed the NET exam of UGC together with my M.A. My status had risen in the university on my getting a gold medal in M.A. Professors looked at me with some affection. Prof. Amresh Tiwari sir was one of them. He kept me with him for my M.Phil. and then for my Ph.D. Thanks to him, I got a job in a famous college of this city. He always loved me like a son, but Vandana's suicide was a setback for him.

The university did not have many Hindu boys or girls.

Prof. Amresh Tiwari used to write poetry at one time but had never faced the fire of sending them for publication. I often went to his home. He had shared these poems with me in quiet, intimate moments. They were love poems, full of the pain of separation and longing.

'I could never gather the courage to propose to the person I loved. She was braver than me.' He was reluctant to call himself a coward. After a third peg, he could take out the collected debris from his heart. This was the technique he had discovered for catharsis.

'We are ready to indulge in all kinds of violent destruction in the name of love, aren't we?'

Amresh sir knew well about my new relationship with Vandana. In spite of her being a 'Jha', he had never opposed it. On the contrary, he had given help in developing this relationship. Maybe he was re-living his past by helping me. But if the past is a wound, then re-living it makes the present sick and impotent. The present and the future can become healthy and bountiful only by cutting themselves off from the past. Amresh sir had not allowed himself to do that.

I started teaching in the college before marrying Vandana. She was an ordinary student. I gave her notes so that she could pass the NET exam of UGC, but she was lazy as well. I was not quite able to grasp this in the beginning, but after our marriage this was a trait that created constant conflict.

Vandana kept on a fight with my mother. Ma expected her to help in the household work. Vandana did try to help but she was not habituated in working. If Ma gave her some work, she took an hour over a five-minute job. Ma would be annoyed with her and attack me. Vandana's father was a chartered accountant and quite wealthy. Vandana, fed up with ma's harsh behaviour, started giving me an earful. I was ground down between my mother and my wife.

My father had not even participated in my marriage. I had asked him to come to the court. 'How will this marriage happen without you, Papa?' I had pleaded.

'Son, I have walked my life-long on the path of Baba Saheb Ambedkar's equality, amity and independence. You are taking advantage of your independence. Am I stopping you? You are free to marry. How, when, with whom—you decide. My duty is simply to help you.'

'But are you fulfilling your duty?'

'What is there for me to do? If I do not want to participate in it, you cannot interfere. It's my right,' he had argued.

'Are you not with me, Papa?'

'No, child, not in this decision of yours. Porridge will dissolve in milk, not in billowing buttermilk. Vandana has a different culture.' He sat down pressing his knees down with his hands.

He did not come for the marriage. Ma came. Women cannot stay annoyed for too long. Amresh sir had signed as the witness from my side. Thus, he had completed his circle.

My father never talked with Vandana, so there was no possibility of any conflict. However, when Vandana did find a ground for difference with him, it became unavoidable to separate.

'Your father is profoundly casteist. He does not forget for a second that I am a Brahmin,' Vandana said irritably one night.

'Why do you need to talk to him at all? He doesn't say anything to me about you,' I said calmly.

'I am his daughter-in-law. He should surely talk to me,' she said and stamped her foot.

'You are also ma's daughter-in-law. How do you get along with her? You are both arguing most of the time. You should study and pass your exams instead of wasting your time on all this.'

'You are all the same. Your Papa has no idea how I had to plead with my mother and father. My mother could not stop crying. I had to step down to this out of love for you.'

'Control yourself, Vandana. If my father is casteist, you and your parents are even more so. And this caste façade has been constructed not by our ancestors but by yours. Now their progenies have to bear the fruit of it.' I also threw water on the embers. She was scalded. After a month, however, we went off to live separately.

I was aware from that day on that now our relationship could not be a simple one any longer. If there is one thing a married couple should avoid, it is insulting each other's family. We had both reached that limit. I did still want to try for a simple relationship. I was also afraid of being proved wrong in my decision in front of others. I did not want my family members to wax sarcastic about my decision, about my marriage. Maybe Vandana had the same fear?

This fear and respect for them made me leave my dear father and mother at the mercy of my younger brother and his wife, and decide to live separately. I wanted peace at any cost. Had Vandana wanted, useless conflict over hundreds of small things could have been avoided. For instance, Ma did not like her wearing skirts and shorts at home. I occasionally smoked a cigarette away from Ma and Papa, and Vandana asserted her equality in this as well. She would get a packet of cigarettes through my younger brother Rinku and then smoke openly. Papa would quietly leave the house, but Ma would confront her. All Vandana wanted was that I stop smoking…was she wrong?

We reached an impasse the night we had a birthday party for her. Mother and father kept to the first floor on their own volition. They did not even glance into the party. Jayant, Firoz, Aslam, Sushil and Vedprakash had come. Jayant and Vedprakash had come with their wives. Jayant and Sushil were always at each other's throats, but we were all close friends. We were all having cold drinks, but Sushil took out half a bottle of Royal Stag from his bag and made two pegs.

'Drinking water is not going to work, mate,' he said.

'So, blood proves strong, after all,' said Jayant, and Sushil gave a loud laugh.

'Yes, my child, my blood is hot. Who's going to join

me?' Sushil looked first at Jayant, who gestured with his eyes towards his wife, wrapped up in conversation on the other side of the room.

'Wife's slave, the son of a bitch,' Sushil said, and looked at Vedprakash, who did what Jayant had done.

'Son of a bitch, they are all castrated,' said Sushil, and everyone laughed.

'Give it to me,' said Aslam, and took the second glass.

'That's like a man,' said Sushil, raising his glass.

'But you'll have to take half, for friendship's sake,' said Aslam, looking at me.

'Fine.' I took the glass and had taken two sips when I found Vandana standing in front of me. She took my glass and smelled it. I felt embarrassed in front of my friends.

'You had alcohol?' she asked.

'A little. Aslam wanted me to.' I tried to avoid trouble.

Vandana put the glass to her mouth and drank it all in one gulp. She didn't stop there but took the bottle kept near Sushil, re-filled her glass and, without mixing water, began to drink. I held her hand.

'Don't do it, Vandana. It'll harm you.'

'You can drink, but we can't because we are women. If we take care of you when you are drunk, can't you take care of us?' She finished the second glass as well. 'Now we are equal. We are not your maidservants.'

I was out of control. The anger had been simmering for many days inside me like lava. I had been quiet, thinking we'll make it right someday. I had no objection to her drinking. If we could drink, she could drink. The point was her reason for drinking. My friends and I were drinking not to tease our wives, but Vandana had done it simply to humiliate me…and I could not contain myself any longer.

Sla-a-a-ap. I gave her a resounding slap on her cheek. 'You don't try to be equal in studying and working. The whole revolution has to be only at home!' I shouted, trembling with anger. Vandana did not move, just stared at me. All the guests were shocked into stillness.

Sla-a-a-ap. Vandana gave me a resounding slap.

Vedprakash and Jayant's wives took her to the next room.

'Sorry, pal,' Sushil apologised and left that instant.

'Wait, Sushil, I'll come with you,' Aslam put his hand on my shoulder and left.

Firoz, Vedprakash and Jayant stood silently near me.

'It happens, buddy,' Firoz gave me a hug.

'I am ruined, Firoz.' His hug made me break down. I began to sob.

'It'll be alright, mate. Husbands and wives are always fighting. Which house doesn't have soot in the kitchen,' Jayant tried to console me.

'You had the drink, she got intoxicated. Don't take it to heart,' Vedprakash said.

They all left. No one ate. Nothing had been cooked. We were going to order in from a restaurant and had not ordered it yet.

'Sorry!' I apologised to her the next morning.

'Sorry!' she also said to me.

I thought the matter was over, but she did not forget it. She told me three or four days later that she had found a flat to rent near the college and we would live there now.

'I'll be able to study there and do my exam preparation,' she gave her reasons. 'You will save on time and transport.'

I told my father different reasons for our living separately, of which the main one was to keep up our love. 'Better than to live together and quarrel is to live apart and love each other.' My father was silent. He kept looking for something in my eyes.

'Be happy. Stay wherever. We are not alone. I have my job,' he said. 'And Chiku and Rinku are with us.'

'Ma and she do not get along,' I said helplessly.

'As long as you two get along, that's all that is important. We are not alone, my child,' he said gravely.

'We will leave day after tomorrow.' I felt like hugging him and crying my heart out.

'It's fine. I'll just worry about you. Here, you were in my sight,' he said, putting his arm around my shoulder.

'Forgive me, Papa.' I touched his feet and broke down.

Father stood quietly. He did not stop me from crying. He stroked my head. When I raised my eyes, I saw that he was also crying. His tears were streaming down soundlessly as if a glacier was melting. I remembered that of the three brothers, Papa maybe loved me the most. Mother would tell me often, 'When you were small, your father said that he looked just like you when he was that age. You are like him in behaviour as well.'

It must have been true. For all his impracticality and emotion, father had never seemed mistaken to me. At the most, he seemed unfamiliar and out of touch with the times. I thought of him as a saint in this time of materialism and consumerism. He had been deceived repeatedly. He had been punished for wrongs he had never committed. But I had never heard him complain about this. He had inherited this quality from Amma.

He had been suspended, for instance, two or three times for taking bribes, but he did not choose to even blame the sanitary inspectors who were responsible for this wrong accusation.

'They have no choice. The sanitary workers have no choice either.' He never said any more. He would tell us that the inspector knew that the sanitary worker did not do the work himself but made someone else do it for a smaller sum. Some money was paid to the inspector who took attendance. There were some workers who had not worked at all, all their lives, and had retired. Most of them had a private business or an extra earning from having the garbage removed from private colonies. 'The whole lot of them are rotten,' Ma would say on hearing all this.

Vandana was fine, except that she was unnecessarily obstinate. She was very possessive, as Firoz put it. She was used to having her say. She was broad-minded, but her broad-mindedness was destroyed by her obstinacy, or maybe it was me who could not control my male chauvinist instincts. This was the same Vandana who was ready to give her life for me.

It was the scary morning of 7 December 1992. M. Phil. classes had been cancelled. We had our lunch in Imran bhai's canteen and lingered on, talking. Those were the days when our friendship was ripening.

Aslam and Jayant were present as well. Firoz went off with Nigar to the Maulana Mehmood Hasan Library, known as Central Library. Sushil had come but left for some work. Firoz, when going, had told us to leave as well.

The atmosphere on campus was tense but looking calm. The university and shops were open, but quiet. The Babri Mosque in Ayodhya had been destroyed just as the 2,000-year-old grand statues of the Buddha in Bamiyan were blown up by cannon. The claims of faith and religion were leaving no space for anyone.

'May the Lord rain catastrophes on them.' Yasmin had given me the news as I entered the university. Her head was covered in her white scarf. 'They will find no place even in hell.' Yasmin came from the nearby Kohinoor neighbourhood. There were many low-class neighbourhoods as well as posh colonies near the university. They were mostly populated by Muslim students and their families. Hindu students lived in the hostel or in colonies away from the university. Hindu-minded people in the city called this place 'Mini Pakistan'. In their vocabulary, this was the second 'Mini Pakistan'. The first one was the neighbourhood with the city's beautiful 600-year-old mosque.

Firoz advised us and left. Yasmin had been the first to give the advice to leave. We kept strolling around. We were confused.

'I am truly pained at this tragedy,' I had said to Aslam. 'But I didn't like what Firoz said, that we should get out of here.'

'I can't believe that they have the guts. I am really shocked,' Vandana had waved her hands and said. 'Religion has driven them crazy.'

'But Aslam, old pal, are we really insecure with you around?' Jayant had asked this.

'As long as Aslam has blood flowing in his veins, no son of a bitch can lay his fingers on you.' Aslam embraced Jayant. This was a speech worthy of the stage but to us, it brought some relief and hope. 'This bastard Firoz is not brave; he is a coward.' We did not quite get his calling Firoz a coward. For us they were both Muslims, just as Vandana or Sushil or I were Hindus for them. What were these identities that came with these names that society had given us?

After September, there was a greenness around the university that was a sight to behold. All kinds of trees were covered with leaves. You couldn't see the branches. The whole city was pretty in the cold of December, but the university was as heart-meltingly beautiful as a babe in arms. The tragedy had struck at the exact time that the university was at its loveliest.

'Come, let's go to the canal,' Vandana proposed.

There was a garden called Krishna Kunj where we often went. It was actually outside our city, on the border of the next state, but adjoined our city.

'I'll take off then,' said Jayant.

'Me too,' said Aslam, holding out his hand to me. 'Don't hang around. The atmosphere is not good. You understand, don't you? Let's go, Jayant, brother.' They both left.

'Rickshaw!' Vandana stopped a rickshaw.

'Where to, brother?' The rikshawalla looked at me.

'Krishna Kunj,' Vandana took her seat.

'At this time?' The rickshawalla's face showed surprise.

Perhaps he understood that his passengers were not Muslims.

'What will you take?' asked Vandana.

'Ten rupees.' He asked double price. Vandana looked at me.

'Come on, are we being taken to the Taj Mahal?' I asked in the made-up intonation of the old city, and he was reduced to pleading.

'Bhai jaan, I'll have to come back without a ride. You are a big person.' He had taken me for a Muslim and Vandana a Hindu, and ours a love affair.

'Going for five or not?' I asked again.

'Give me seven,' he pleaded again.

'Oh, come on.' I sat, looking at Vandana. Her eyes were full of praise.

It was three in the afternoon. We reached Krishna Kunj in 10 minutes. It was a busy place. Couples of all kinds had each found their corner or tree, and were in a world of their own—a world without a temple or a mosque or a church or a monastery. This world only had a little flame of love that burned impeccably. It remained unwavering on Vandana and my entering it, just as an actual flame remains untouched no matter who is in the room.

'Will we ever be fulfilled?' Vandana leaned against a tree trunk.

'...' I began to look away. I simply did not know how to make romantic talk. She was used to asking questions and giving her own answers.

'You'll see, we will. We will be one,' she said, resting her head on my chest. 'My dream is that I die in your arms.'

I just kept stroking her hair. She kept talking. The script was from the films, but at that time did not strike me as theatrical. I neither liked nor disliked Vandana in the beginning. Her face had no attraction for me. She was fair, with an average face and figure. Her eyes were somewhat large and protruding. Her sharp nose and thin lips still did not bestow beauty on her. Her face did have an attractiveness because it was small and triangular. Anyway, who holds back if a woman professes love to a man.

Slowly, I grew to love her, for which the credit went not to her body but her talk. She was so crazy about me it seemed she had no one else in the world she loved. Did I really start loving her or was it my male ego's delusion that a woman was devoted to me body and soul? Whether it was ego or delusion or love, it grew so strong that I could not stay without her for a minute. That was the beginning of her rule over me. Now, she began to throw tantrums. She would not speak for two full days, and the wonder was that she could stay without talking…but I would almost die. Had she made me addicted to her using her devotion and love as a drug? At that time, I could not be analytical.

One time, we quarreled over something and she completely stopped talking to me. I was at a loss as to what to do. I could not eat for two days and survived on water. Jayant told Vandana about my food strike on Saturday and Sunday, and Vandana had come running. She rushed to hug me, in broad daylight, in the middle of the university faculty. Both of us burst out crying, and then ate together. Was this love or the madness of youth, or the madness of love itself?

'How much do you love me, Vanjha?' The magic of Krishna Kunj could sometimes bring words to my mouth. I called her, Vandana Jha, Vanjha.

'As much as a person loves salt,' she said, raising her head from my chest and looking into my eyes.

These were our first days together and she was restless for me all the time…but things changed in six months. I began to feel that she did not love me as she used to, but now it was impossible for me to forget her. Either I had lost my mind or she was truly skilled in making someone a slave. I was like a honey bee drowning in her sweet words. You cannot be so analytical about love anyway. Vandana seemed to know, however, that in love as in politics, one was victorious with a wait and watch policy.

We forgot all about time while at Krishna Kunj. We even forgot that the only road back to the city went straight through the university. It was dark. The colourful, musical fountains of the Kunj had made us forget the dark night. Another couple that I recognised left the Kunj at the same time. It was a Hindu girl who came in the morning in our University Special bus. Her name was Tanvi Arora, I think. She would get on at Lajpat

Nagar and off at the Fine Arts Faculty, from what I remember. Her boyfriend was a Muslim, not a Hindu. Vandana and I had met him with Aslam a few times. He lived in the Maroon House Hostel, and was from Aslam's hometown, Amroha. He called himself Danish Amrohi.

There were two groups of Bihar and U.P. boys in the hostel who often fought with each other. Sometimes, the groups would fight in the hostels the whole night through—we had even heard of some students getting killed. Both the groups were of Muslim boys. Muslims and Hindus did not fight with each other. The fights were on regional differences, not religious ones. The point is that if people are looking for a reason to fight, there is no dearth of causes. In my alma mater for my B.A., the quarrel had been between castes. There were Jat villages around and Jats dominated in my college. The boys from our colony had a ready front against them because they were quite skilled in the use of a knife.

'Vanjha, did you recognise them?' I asked as he started his motorcycle. Danish had shown no sign of recognition or familiarity.

'Yes, he had met us once with Aslam, right?' she said with indifference.

'Not once, many times. That was Danish. He lives in Maroon Hostel with Aslam,' I tried to remind her.

Vandana was pretending to not remember. Danish was

a handsome and well-built young man. He had a girlish innocence and the body of a Pathan. He was someone difficult to forget after a meeting. I'd say that for women, it was impossible. Then why was Vandana pretending she could not recognise him? Because women and girls cheat their men by pretending to be extra virtuous in front of them. They probably understand the ways of the world better.

'Yes, now I remember,' she said. 'We had tea together, didn't we, in Imran bhai's canteen?'

'He is very emotional and hot-tempered.'

'Then he must not be very smart.'

'That I don't know, but it is a fact that stupid people bring trouble on themselves and put others into trouble also.'

'Guruji, how should we recognise such people?' Vandana said theatrically, joining her hands.

'Their most visible trait, my child, is that they think themselves the smartest and the rest of the world stupid,' I said. And we both laughed.

'Who was the girl with him?' Vandana asked between her laughter.

'She is a girl from Punjab. She lives in that refugee neighbourhood on Sadar Road, in Shahid Lajpat Vihar. She is often on the U-Special with me.'

'Hindu?'

I nodded. In fact, I knew a lot about Danish. He had

land in Amroha. He was much respected in his community because his ancestors had come from some special part of Arabia. Firoz had told me that he was utterly emotional and hot-tempered, and could even kill in the name of religion. He boasted of acquiring 'merit' with his conquest of Hindu girls. It was not news to me. Many Hindu and Sikh boys said the same thing about Muslim girls. Whether Hindu, Sikh, Muslim or Christian—in all cases, the victim of the men's fire were women.

It was only 5:30 in the evening, but it was dark. We asked the rickshawallas outside the Kunj to take us but they were from the adjoining state and refused to enter our city. We kept walking as we talked. There was almost no traffic. Barely one truck and one car passed us in all that time. There were huts alongside the canal, and the rising smoke from them announced that food was on its way. The breeze brought the smell of biryani from one of the homes.

We were walking on a footpath next to the canal. The cold had increased. Vandana had tucked her hands into her jeans' pockets, and I had pulled my fists into the sleeves of my sweater. The total walking distance from the Kunj to the university was 20 minutes at the most. We had covered half the distance when a group of five or six boys passed. We paid no attention to them but 20 steps or so later, Vandana said that they were following us. 'Don't turn around,' I said. 'Pretend you don't see them.' Then I remembered that all the homes around us were Muslim. On the right was the canal and on the left were the homes. Then I remembered in a flash all the events that had occurred since the morning.

Firoz's warning, Yasmin's condemnation to hell, Sushil's leaving, Asma saying, 'Leave soon, the atmosphere is bad'. I remembered Danish's aloofness as he started his motorcycle. I figured that the people following us were surely armed. I was getting ready to fight, knowing that if we didn't, we would be killed. I was worried about Vandana. I calculated that if we ran very fast, we would have to run for 10 minutes straight. Vandana would not be able to.

'Walk faster,' Vandana whispered. She had taken her hand out of her pocket and gripped mine. 'They are just behind us.'

We began to walk faster. We had hardly walked a few steps, and it seemed as if we had walked miles and our destination was receding. Our legs were like stone.

'Stop, you motherfucker…' One of the men caught hold of my hand from the back and abused me.

'What's the problem? Why are you talking like this?' I glared at him.

'What is your name?' He had closed my mouth with his fingers. Behind him I could see the twinkling lights of Krishna Kunj.

'We study here at the university,' Vandana said, removing his hand. 'Mind your own business.'

'Study, sure, and conduct their love affairs.' He took out a little knife. It was the kind of knife that fruit sellers kept to slice their guavas or bananas. But in the tension of the evening, even that knife made an impact. The other boys of the group were standing quietly behind the one with the knife. The one with the knife had on a Pathani kamiz and pajama. He even looked like a hawker.

'Tell me your name, you bastard, or I'll knife you!' he roared.

'Please don't be abusive, bhai-jaan…My name is Nigar. We are Muslims too.' Vandana showed him the locket around her neck that had been given to her by Nigar a few days back. 'We live in Kohinoor Nagar…you can check up…he is my fiancé.' Vandana held my wrist.

'Name?' His eyes had a combination of belief and unbelief. They were all swaying between the two.

'Firoz.' Again, Vandana was the one who answered.

'Please step aside,' he said with attitude. 'Pull down your pants. We'll find out in a second.' He had a smile now, full of mischief, but enough to make us scared.

He had hardly spoken when Vandana suddenly kicked him hard on his crotch. Her aim was so precise that the knife fell from his hands and he rolled over like a sack of potatoes. He had not been prepared for such an attack in the least.

'Run!' Vandana took hold of my hand and screamed. The boys as well as me were standing in surprise. We began to run towards the university. Contrary to my expectations, Vandana was running quite fast. Her jeans made it easy for her to take long strides. That's why men prefer saris and long skirts on their women, I suppose.

'Catch them, catch them! Kill them, kill them! They are unbelievers, the bastards!' The other four boys were lifting the kicked boy. Two chased us as well, but by that time we had run far. As we were running, a rickshaw passed by us, also going fast.

'Climb on, brother,' he slowed down.

Vandana jumped on immediately. I got on running. He cycled fast and we could not see the boys anymore.

'Things are bad, brother.' He had now slowed down.

Vandana's hands were trembling. I was also nervous but held her hands tight. In spite of the cold, we were bathed in sweat.

'It's over. Don't be afraid now,' I said, panting.

'Yes, it was frightening,' she said softly.

'But he'll remember your kick all his life,' I tried to smile.

'Are you Hindus, brother?' the rickshawalla asked suddenly.

'Why?' We were afraid again at this new turn.

'Nothing. Those boys were shouting "Unbelievers!", that's why.'

'Yes,' I gathered up the courage to say.

On hearing this, he slowed down further. We could see the B.Ed. faculty of the university ahead. The Kohinoor Nagar market was deserted. It was chock-a-block at this time on other days. Huge woks of milk, pots of mutton biryani—the world's aromas would have filled the market. Shops would be full of *jalebis*, *imartis*, *kachoris*, *paan*. Seeing the busy market deserted, it seemed like a different place.

'Things are bad. You should not have been out at a time like this.' The man's attitude had changed.

'We had no idea,' Vandana said.

'On top of which, you are wearing jeans,' he muttered angrily. 'You'll die and get me killed as well.' He had almost stopped the rickshaw. 'Please get off. The rioters will bury us right here.'

'Be kind to us, brother.' Vandana had understood from his accent that he was from Mithila district. I could also tell, from the way he exchanged 'r' for 'd' and 'd' for 'r'. Vandana herself used to speak like that, and repeated corrections had cured her.

'Impossible,' he said.

'The whole place is burning. You are wearing those kinds of clothes as well. Whoever doesn't know, will know at a glance.' He was hitting the pedal with dead feet.

We were passing through Kohinoor market. Suddenly a rock hit the front tyre of the rickshaw. It had been thrown from a roof. The rock made a huge noise. The dogs wandering around started barking. Hearing them, the dogs of other neighbourhoods started barking as well. We all felt worried; even if there was nothing, we all had a sense of what could happen.

'We will give you 50 rupees,' Vandana said.

'It's dangerous. What will I do with 50 rupees if I am not alive? My daughter is sick at home. I had come out for her medicine.'

'Fine, we'll give you 300 rupees. Get us out of here.'

I believed that the offer of an unthought-of unreal amount broke a man's determination. By chance, I had 300 rupees in my pocket from a tuition fee payment from a student.

'I can't promise anything. Let's try…if someone stops you, say you are Muslims.' Saying which, he started hitting the pedals hard again.

We sat tight on the rickshaw. It was racing the wind. It was 15 minutes to Ranbaxy Eye Hospital. This hospital marked the end of 'Mini Pakistan' and the border with 'Hindustan'. The roads were deserted. The library and canteen which were otherwise alive till late at night lay deserted. Two government buses had been put to flames on the main road; they were still smoking. We had not sensed any smoke in Krishna Kunj.

'Here you are, brother,' he said, stopping at the gate of the hospital.

'Here,' I said, putting 300 rupee notes in his hand. 'Thank you very much.'

'We will never forget this favour by you,' Vandana added.

'No, I can't take 300. Give me 20 in change.' He put the notes back in Vandana's hands. 'Honesty is a big thing. I'll have to answer to Allah on the Day of Judgement.'

'No, no, you are going to have to keep this,' and Vandana forcibly put the notes into his pocket.

We continued on our way. The place was active like other days. The market was glittering. The police had made a front. Fat Punjabi women were gobbling down *gol gappas* with their naughty children. Lit up cars lined the streets. The rickshawalla went on to a medicine shop, no doubt to get his daughter's medicine.

Why did the same Vandana who was ready to die for me in 1992 kill herself in 1994? I was never able to figure it out. Were the two Vandanas the same? It was unimaginable that the Marxist Vandana should have transformed into the casteist Vandana.

I swung between the past and the present.

CHAPTER FIVE

Vandana, Gone

We did save on transport and time from moving closer to the college, but a week after that Vandana became her same self again. The soil has to be fertilised by mutual tolerance, after all, for relationships to blossom. Trying to pull each other down and crush one another is poisonous.

'Why don't you try for the Civil Services?' Vandana asked me one evening.

'No, I don't want to be a civil servant,' I had replied. 'I don't see a civil servant's ability within myself.'

'How can a "Gold Medalist" and "Meritorious Student" say this about himself?' She decided to be sarcastic.

'That's an individual opinion. Why don't you try for the Services?' I asked in return. 'I love to teach. Each to their own work.'

'Why don't you just say that you are lazy?' she got upset. 'You should be ashamed, trying to live on a woman's earnings.'

I did not react to her rudeness. I had got used to her habits. She wanted a quarrel and I did not want to disturb my peace. I started to change to go out.

'Where do you think you are going?' She jumped up and held my hand.

'I have some work,' I pulled my hand away.

'Work. What work? I am not one of those women who sit at home cooking and wait for their husband's return. My foot!' She stamped her feet.

'Please, Vanjha. Don't fight all the time. Cook if you feel like it. Don't cook if you don't. I'll come back and cook. But I've done my turn washing the dishes.'

She sat silently on the bed watching me. I put on my shoes and my favourite perfume.

'What is the work you are going on?' Her voice had a bitterness.

I was quiet. I myself did not know where I was going. How could I tell her my destination? My destination was lost anyway. I was just wandering about. All I could say was that I could not bear to sit at home and have insults hurled at me. I could understand that she was used to dominating, and could not break the habit now. She was the oldest daughter in her home and this was her behaviour there. To give her any answer at all was to invite a quarrel.

'What is the work? Tell me before going.' She stood up.

'I am going to Amresh sir's place. It's been a while,' I tried to be evasive.

'I'll come too.' She sounded stubborn.

'Whatever for?' I stammered nervously.

'Then why don't you acknowledge that you are going to meet your lover?' She misinterpreted my nervousness. 'I understand your tricks...'

'That's a lot of nonsense. Even you know that to have a relationship with you is enough,' I tried to be sarcastic but she did not notice.

'This blank call that came just now must have been some girlfriend of yours whom you gave a time and then forgot. You are a man of pleasure.'

There had been an increase in blank calls on the phone at home for some days now. She was suspicious of me because whenever she lifted the phone, no one answered. Sometimes there was a woman on the other side who had dialed our number by mistake. Sometimes there were men. But Vandana always claimed that I was being called. The men's calls were supposed to be the pimp or middleman's. I understood full well that this was her new prescription for controlling me.

My silence was a more fatal weapon than speech. I was silent.

'You are not leaving.' She came forward and started unbuttoning my shirt.

'What is this, Vanjha? Leave me in peace somewhere at least,' I said angrily.

'Yes, of course. It's me who does not let you live in peace. That is why you keep running off outside. Why not just say that you are fed up with me.' Her tone had changed.

'Why are you putting on this act? Get out of my way,' I pushed her gently.

'I am putting on an act? I will eat poison and kill myself one day, then you will know how much I love you.' She made a face.

I knew that she did love me a lot. She also knew that I loved her. What was it, then, between us that kept us apart? Was it the aggressive face of love, in which all that was important was control of the other person? When there was no space left of respect for each other's feelings? Was this now only the age-old game of power between male and female? The threat of suicide was but one technique in that game.

'Don't talk about dying, Vanjha,' I said, taking her in my arms. 'I won't be able to live without you.' I had become emotional on hearing of her killing herself.

Now she was smiling. I changed my plans and got out of my clothes. I cooked that evening. She kept studying the whole time, just as I had been asking her to do. That night, after many nights, went well. She did not make excuses or fight. None of the stomach ache, back ache, headache or other aches that she gave as an excuse for turning over and falling asleep.

'Your needs are more than I can satisfy. You need another woman as well,' she said resting on my shoulder, covered with perspiration. She kept playing with the hair on my chest.

This was also a face of hers—the face that reminded me of the Vandana of 7 December 1992. Now this face was visible only every five or six months. She was her old self in the morning. I made breakfast and woke her up as I left for college.

She had been victorious in love, and was now deprived of the pleasure of defeat. She imagined that love was a simple project and instead of cutting out the power play, was increasing it. This was at the heart of the tension in our relationship, which she refused to acknowledge.

Our days were passing thus. Meanwhile, I developed a bad habit. I was trying to spend my free time outside home to be free of the arguing, and one road to freedom led to Sushil's parties. I don't even know when I became a permanent fixture at these gatherings. The parties meant drinking. I could now sleep peacefully because of the drinks. Vandana would keep ranting and I, immune to the rants, would snore away.

'Promise me that after today you will never drink again,' Vandana said, putting my hand on her head one night.

'I don't believe in these reactionary things.' Drunk, I had swapped her hand away. I had taken a decision that when she did not accept anything I said, I would pay her back in the same coin. I would also live as I liked.

'The drinking will ruin your health, why don't you understand?' She began to cry.

'What do you care? The biggest enemy of my health is you.' Drunk, I could not control myself.

'If you don't listen, I am going to kill myself, just look out,' she said, trembling with anger. She had picked up a knife.

'You are a coward, and you are trying to scare me. You will never kill yourself. You are a parasite, and will drink my blood like a leech all your life.' Thanks to the drinking, I had become used to rudeness myself.

'To work and earn is not in your genes, you bastard Brahmins who have always begged for alms like beggars.' I took the knife from her hand and threw it away. 'If it had been another woman, she would have washed my feet with her tears and thanked her good fortune.'

She cried through the night. I could not then see the horrible impact of my drinking. The short-term effect I enjoyed was that Vandana had stopped saying bitter things to me. If she did say something to me in the morning, I would use the same words to give her hell at night. The tables had turned now.

There was a story Sushil told of a stubborn woman who insisted on doing the opposite of what her husband said. One day they went for a swim in the river on the woman's suggestion. 'Don't go that side. The current is strong,' the man advised her. The woman went exactly to that side. As she was being swept away by the current, the man held out his hand. 'Hold my hand or you will be swept away.' The wife said, 'No, I won't, and I won't be swept away.' And away she was swept.

In men's gatherings like this one, women were given respect. But drinking had distorted my judgement, and I had begun to take our terrible situation lightly.

It was New Year Eve's party. I was getting ready to go. We had just returned from window shopping in Central market.

'Don't go out today,' Vandana had said invitingly.

'Why?'

'Oh, just like that. I feel like staying together this evening.'

'But I have promised them.'

'Phone them and say no.'

'A commitment is a commitment.'

'I mean nothing to you,' she began to cry.

'Of course, you do. We just went out together. Why don't you call Jayant or Nigar's wife over?' I was already on my way out.

'If you go now, you will see my dead face on coming back,' Vandana said in tears.

'Why make these empty threats? You are a real coward.' I had thought of it as the daily empty threat. I said it lightly with a laugh.

'Today I won't let you go.' She got up and put her arms around my neck.

'Please don't be stubborn, Vanjha.' I held her. I found it impossible to argue with her for long. I did not want to cancel my going but did not want to see her sad either. 'I'll come back soon. Please.'

'No. We have already decided.'

This was not the voice of love. Instead of sweetness, there was steel. It was not a request but an order. She was not my Vanjha but the dictatorial Vandana Jha. Her voice and the feel of her order made me squirm inside.

'All right,' I said with resignation. 'What should we cook?'

'Rice and dal.'

'No, shahi paneer,' I had a plan.

'Alright.'

'I'll make it. You make the dal and rice. Arhar dal.' I pressed her hand. 'Let me get the paneer.'

'Alright. Get some yogurt as well.'

I said yes and departed. I looked at the time. Eight o'clock. I took an auto, and at 8:20 I was at Sushil's party. Sushil had received the letter of appointment to the Indian Police Service just a week back; he was about to leave for training. The party was from his side. We were all waiting to see him in his uniform. Jayant had been appointed in the Allied Services once again, and yet again, he was not going to join. He was determined to get into the IPS.

'Ah, the maharaja has arrived,' Sushil saw me enter and threw a barb. 'Welcome, welcome.'

'Bastard slave of the wife,' Aslam gave me a hug. 'Jayant, brother, he is your companion.'

'Leave it, pal,' I said, sitting down.

I shook hands with Jayant and Sushil. There were three new faces at the party holding their glasses in their hands. I shook hands with the three. Firoz was holding his beer bottle in one corner. The two of us rarely shook hands, but we depended the most on each other. We knew each other's secrets. Maybe we were so close that shaking hands was a pointless civility.

'Vedprakash did not come?' I asked, noticing his absence.

'I did not call him,' Sushil said.

'Why?' I lifted the glass that Sushil had made for me.

'That Brahmin hates me,' Sushil said. 'I am a Valmiki.' There was no bitterness in his voice, just amusement. He was smiling as he said it.

Sushil's full name was Sushil Valmiki. His father had passed away when he was eleven or twelve years old. He worked as a sanitary worker in the City Municipality and while cleaning the sewers one day, he had died. His wife had been given his job at the Municipality on compensatory grounds. Papa had helped them too. Because she was a woman, Sushil's mother had got a street sweeper's job.

Educated till class X, Sushil's mother had grown up in this very city and was not prepared to take it. She did not want to sweep the streets. Her father worked in the Municipality as a doorman as well. Her father and mine did some running around on her behalf and, finally, she was appointed as a water woman.

'If it's the work that gives us the label of "dirty", then why do that work?', she says till today. 'Clean up the city and make yourself "dirty"; that is what is bringing the community down.'

She made sure of Sushil and his brother Vinod's education. It was the fruit of her labour that he was now a member of the nation's highest service. Papa called it the victory of democracy.

'It's only possible in a democracy that the son of a cobbler become the President and the son of a sanitary worker, Sushil, become a Collector. Democracy makes people equal,' he said upon hearing the news.

Vedprakash did not take much to Sushil, or ever come to his house. 'I don't care for Sushil's caste,' he had told me one day. 'I am repulsed by this work, even though I know that I touch my own shit daily. I try to tell myself that I don't care, but it doesn't work. If his father had not been doing the sewer cleaning, it would have been fine.' He sounded full of pity.

'But he has been dead for a year, and his mother does not do a sweeping job. His house is spotless. Have you seen it?' I asked him.

'I cannot persuade myself, old pal. It just doesn't work. I have no problem with you or Jayant. Jayant is a Jatav, and in our village we do not sit with Jatavs. I have not seen all that. I was born in the city; I don't know what the Jatavs do in the village. But in the city, I have certainly seen Valmikis clean sewers and remove garbage.' He was quiet for a moment. 'You can't swallow a fly once you have spotted it.'

Maybe Vanjha was battling with similar doubts in her head. Sushil, Jayant, Aslam, Nigar and Firoz must have been battling with them too. Amresh sir likewise, and my father and I as well. We had not accepted defeat, but neither was the fight over. Amma had perhaps tasted victory. She had conquered her desires. She had tamed the lion and was riding it.

'We've had two pegs each. Finish up. How long will you nurse your glass?' Sushil's voice was sweet.

Aslam held out his glass, 'Sushil, mate, give us one.'

'You have not introduced us,' I told Sushil signalling towards the three new faces.

'Oh, sorry, pal. These are three new friends, from this same city.' Sushil put his hand on the closest one's knee.' They have also passed their Civil Service exams this year.'

'Great. Congratulations…but how did you meet?' I asked.

'Long live the Jatav lobby!' Sushil looked in Jayant's direction, laughing.

'Meaning?'

'Meaning that our people work in government offices too. Jayant has a family friend who he asked for the names of those who are the Reserved candidates from our city. That's how we got their names. Jayant went ahead and invited them to this party.'

'Jayant, you did well,' I told Jayant.

'Well indeed…how can we survive without unity. I am not like Sushil, cursing caste day and night.' He looked at Sushil. 'His very opponents have changed now. They used to be upper castes, now the opponents are the Jatavs. That's what they wanted and that's what he's doing.'

'Bastard, you're not trying to understand what I am saying.' Sushil put his glass down. 'I don't condemn the whole Jatav caste. I am just put off by those Jatavs who practice untouchability with us. They are all hidden Vedprakashs. How many Jatavs are like you?'

'Many.'

'Very few. 10 or 20 are not going to be able to end the hostility of thousands of years.'

'Not 10 or 20, but there are tens of thousands of us who have love and equality for the Valmikis. But the Valmikis are themselves weighed down by their self-consciousness of backwardness, inferiority and discrimination. They have to pull themselves out of this trap.' Jayant spoke sharply.

'Hold on, hold on.' I knew that Sushil would now get louder.

We were friends for the last many years. We had none of these thoughts when we were students. Once we all got jobs, we somehow developed caste consciousness as well. 'Sushil, old pal, are you going to introduce your new friends or just keep fighting?'

'It's Jayant, spoiling one's mood.'

'How am I to blame? You are the one who started off "Long live the Jatav lobby"!'

'This is…'

'Avinash Gautam.' The new young man interrupted Sushil. 'I had not told you my full name earlier, Sushilji. I thought that surnames between one's own people are immaterial.'

'I am Birpal Singh Jatav.' This young man, unlike Avinash, had no softness in his voice. His was a dry and hard voice, that of the city's neighbouring villages. Birpal extended his hand towards me.

'My father works as a mochi in the village, even now. We are full-fledged chamars,' he laughed. I felt that he had added Jatav for our benefit, and that his name must be just Birpal Singh.

'Are you from the Kishangarh side?' I asked. That side saw the beginning of farmhouses. They were Gujjar villages.

'No, there is a village beyond Kishangarh called Mango Khurd. Have you heard of it?'

'Yes, indeed. I went there once. Some Dalit doctors had put up a free camp for the Dalits of the village,' I said. 'I have a distant uncle who is a doctor.'

'That's right. About six or seven months ago.'

'Exactly.' I looked at the third young man.

'Myself K. Rajesh Kumar,' said the man when he noticed me looking at him.

Everyone in the gathering fell silent on hearing this name. Was it because, like me, they were unable to guess his caste? His caste was impossible to know from his name. Why did he not make it easier for us? What caste could he be? That was the only question on my mind. Was that so for Sushil, Jayant, and the others as well? Were they all silent because an anonymous face had appeared in a gathering full of clearly marked castes, and because this anonymity had to be punctured? Were Aslam and Firoz thinking something similar as well? Did the name Rakesh unravel our nationalist consciousness? We, who were against caste, now were keen to know his caste. We, who put up camps for Dalits. We, who wanted to knit together different castes under one Dalit banner—why did we need to know who he was?

'Are you a South Indian?' Marking his tanned features, I tried to make a dishonest attempt at getting my caste question answered.

'No, we are from U.P., and I was born in this very city.' He seemed to guess at my dishonesty. He gave us no help.

'Jayant, I know you won't agree, but the greatest benefits from Reservations have been taken by the Jatavs,' said Sushil.

'This is true.' K. Rakesh's agreement gave Sushil support.

'In every office and every administrative unit, they are there. Clearly, the Jatavs are a lobby.' Sushil's tone was sarcastic.

'What's there to disagree with? We got an education. We followed the philosophy of Baba Saheb Ambedkar, "Study, be united, fight", and we could come forward.' Jayant's voice was bitter too. 'We did not forbid Valmikis or any other caste from studying, or following Ambedkar's thoughts. Now if someone just wants to fight for the rights to sweep, sure, let them fight.'

'Chamars are certainly not going to do us any favours.' Sushil became bitter too. 'As for rights to sweep, hear this Jayant, we prefer to sweep and earn than to beg and eat.'

'I feel that one should not expect Jatavs to do anything for other castes, as we should not from Brahmins,' K. Rakesh said.

'Why?' I asked.

'That has been my experience,' said K. Rakesh.

'And will Jats, Yadavs, Kayasthas and Bhumihars help other castes?' I asked again.

'I have no experience of that. But I do of Brahmins and Jatavs,' K. Rakesh replied.

'Well, I feel that no caste helps another caste when there are huge numbers from that same caste seeking help. Not just Brahmins and Jatavs, but all the other forward and backward castes of North India behave the same way.' I looked at K. Rakesh.

It was clear from his talk so far that he was from a non-Jatav caste.

'Jatavs are not in the same situation in South India as they are in the North. In Maharashtra, it is the Mahars who are in that situation.' I looked at Rakesh carefully.

'Mahars, Matangs and Mangs are more the untouchables in Maharashtra than the Chamars. It was the Chamars who opposed Baba Saheb Ambedkar the most—is this not true?' Sushil said with annoyance.

'It's not true. Baba Saheb was not opposed by the Jatavs. Sushil, try to understand this conspiracy. History allows us to re-interpret…do it.' I spoke with heat though I knew that Sushil was not wrong.

'But we know from many Marathi authors that in Maharashtra the Chamars joined Jagjivan Ram to weaken Baba Saheb's movement,' K. Rakesh said.

'A writer is not a God; they are people like us. They have their limits, weaknesses, low values. They have their prejudices and self-interest. Whether it's Baba Saheb, or Jagjivan Ram, or Jagannath Pahariya…all of them are important people. They have all taught us about inequality. We may compare their achievements, but to remove one and put another on top is wrong.' Jayant nodded as I said this.

'I agree with you. They are different kinds of legacies for us,' said Avinash Gautam.

'And Sushil, mate, you are going into the upper echelons of service now. Fix your mind on the perspective that you will work for all castes. Of course, you will still be held responsible for your own *biradari*.' I patted his knee. 'If Valmikis are making a mistake, it's the same mistake that Chamars in Maharashtra made, according to you, against the Mahars. It is a mistake to silence hopeful minor castes trying to make their voices heard against a dominant caste. The Brahmins are helpless because of their small numbers, so they have always tried to silence other minor castes in front of the dominant castes. It's a fight of numbers—the major versus the minor castes. The major castes happen in places to be Jatavs, in places Mahars and elsewhere, Malas and Doms. This fight cannot continue in a democratic set-up.'

'"There's a new spring, ready to bubble in the stony bowers. There's a new era, waiting anxiously to turn itself around." Brothers, there are Muslims, too, in this gathering with you.' Aslam's reciting a verse made everyone laugh.

'Absolutely. When did we consider you separate?' said Jayant.

'It was you who could save us from Muslims in College.'

'Says Hafiz, "My language is the language of love, not Hindi, or Urdu, or Hindustani." Jayant bro, that's the language I know.'

Aslam could rain down a shower of verses after the third peg.

'Excellent, excellent!' shouted Birpal. He had also drunk a lot.

'Friends, Hindus have been defeated by their caste. There are castes within castes within castes, like a banana flower. Once upon a time, a faqir thought, "Both the Brahmin and I ask for alms, and he gets his with respect and I get mine with a scolding…" So he shaved his head and kept a holy tuft, put a red mark on his forehead, wore a dhoti and set out to seek alms. That day he received extra food and no scolding. So, he began to do it every day. One day he was sitting in a row of Brahmins to eat and his neighbor asked him what kind of a Brahmin he was. He had heard somewhere that Gaur Brahmins are superior, so he said "Gaur Brahmin." The neighbor then asked, "What kind of Gaur?" The faqir spat out in spite of himself, "Allah, Gaurs also have kinds of Gaurs?"' Aslam's anecdote made us all laugh.

'Aslam is right. Hindus are unequal on principle.' Jayant was doubling over with laughter. He was laughing the longest of all of us.

The conversation kept moving on. We dealt with society,

religion, politics, and moved on to tales of past loves and hidden moments with them. None of us could be bettered. None of us had had less than four or five affairs. Do girls or women also get together and pass time telling stories of their past loves? Are these stories true at all, or are they just boastful figments of the imagination? Apart from the story of Vandana, my stories had all been stolen from others or made up… dressed up to seem mine. Were others telling similarly false and made-up stories? And if they were true, did every young man desire only an untouched virgin girl? And did all young women similarly want untouched virgin men?

Avinash, Birpal Singh, Rakesh, Firoz and Jayant left around 10 or 10:30. Aslam, Sushil and I kept eating and drinking. I did not realise how time passed. One minute was left for the New Year. Sushil turned off the lights.

'Happy New Year!' shouted Aslam on the dot.

'And to you!' We all greeted each other and turned on the lights.

'Let's go,' I told Aslam.

The three of us descended the stairs. Sushil's mother was sleeping, or pretending to sleep so that the young men could be allowed to leave quietly. Mothers—they love and they spoil.

'Where is your motorcycle?' Sushil asked Aslam.

'It was not starting so I left it,' Aslam said.

'You've done me in, Aslam brother. I don't know about

getting an auto at this hour.' I was no longer drunk.

'If we don't get one, we'll sleep right here,' he replied.

'Vandana is alone at home, pal.' Aslam smiled at hearing the worry in my voice.

'She'll hardly be alone,' said Sushil. 'She'll be with her anger. Reach home and she'll roast you alive, you bastard.'

We kept searching an hour for an auto but could not find one. They were all full. Exhausted, we came back to Sushil's house.

I awoke at 7:00 and woke Aslam up. We got ready and set out. I had persuaded Aslam to come to my place with me. He resisted but agreed. He was also afraid of Vandana's sharp speech. He always said that if she were his wife, he would have tamed her; and if she did not get tamed, he would divorce her. I could not do that. I loved her. I was only aggrieved by her stubbornness. I knew that she could not live a second without me. I had read in her diary just a few days ago that she hurt me without meaning to, and was herself helpless with her habits.

It was 8:00 when we reached home. I felt worried when I saw a crowd underneath. Aslam and I had barely moved forward when the police jeep standing there left, and behind it an ambulance.

'Oh god, where were you? Your wife committed suicide.' A neighbour ran up and gave me the news.

'Aslam!' I tried to hold on to his arm but fainted and fell to the ground.

The neighbour and Aslam picked me up and brought me to the side, and I slowly regained consciousness. I remembered everything. I wanted to cry but the strange thing was that I could not. Was it the false pride of manhood that prevented me from crying in front of so many people?

The next six months were the most humiliating and challenging days of my life. At first, there was just the pain of the loss of Vandana. Then it was intensified by the accusation that I had pushed her towards suicide. An elephant-like weight fell on me. A single page of Vandana's diary was responsible for a six-month term in jail. She had written that I had beaten her when drunk. On the basis of that, I was called an alcoholic and wife-beater. My character was stained, my illegitimate relations were bounced around. I lost my job. I could not even see Amresh sir. He himself had been unable to understand the event. I could not figure out how Vandana, who was so afraid of death, had taken poison and killed herself? She had not left a suicide note. People had told me that she was found at the front door of the house. The door was open. She must have waited for me, and thought that I would come back in time to save her. That did not happen. She left me, alone.

After six months in prison, I learnt a new lesson in life, maybe the same lesson that Amma had also gradually learnt, the lesson of accepting events—of not giving up, of not complaining, of moving on and living life in new ways. The case went on for three years, and I was let go 'without prejudice' at the end.

I had a chance to see the new faces of old friends over these three years. My new friends were criminals who had been indicted for murder and fraud. I saw the faces of these criminals that were unseen by the world. Most of them were emotional and angry people. They had committed crimes because they had taken small things to be big ones. One had murdered his girlfriend and another, his girlfriend's lover. One had killed his wife only because he had suspected her of relations with another. He had not been able to give the court any proof of her infidelity, and had not been granted a divorce. He had lost his mind.

Inside them, somewhere, they were all beautiful people. How had a responsible father, a crazed lover, become criminals? Because of caste, or religion, or the law? Could these have been bigger than a person's life? Could human beings who laughed innocently or cried from heartbreak become criminals? In these six months I investigated every bit of my life. I was surrounded by insanity for six months, fought it and came out triumphant.

I found a new life, as Amma had found after dadaji's death.

Then Sangita came into my life. I had not managed to

forget Vandana, but had resigned myself to her death as an accident. The resignation had given me strength to live, fight, and move ahead. I would never forget Vandana…never be able to live without her…never love another…is how I used to think. Gradually, however, time placed many healing layers on me, and I did not fight that.

Father insisted on my getting remarried. Sudesh chacha brought the proposal; he was a doctor. His wife was also a doctor. The two of them were associated with Bamsafe. They put up free camps in the slums with other Dalit doctors. Sangita was from a batch junior to them. She was perhaps distantly related to my aunt. They were both from Ludhiana district in the Punjab. Sangita had done her medical degree from our city. On hearing her father's name, my father had said, 'He is one of our Chamars, and lives in the Cantt. No matter where he goes, a member of your caste will be found out.'

Sangita's family were Buddhists. In our family, my mother definitely kept some Hindu fasts. Papa had dropped all faith in Hinduism but had been unable to move towards any other religion. If anyone asked him, he always said he was a Buddhist. But he had not actually converted. My mother was quite clear that she was a Hindu. Papa's was a strange situation. He did not consider himself a Hindu and went to the Buddhist monastery every Sunday. He knew the Panchsheel and Trisharan by heart but did not feel as if that satisfied him.

'The son dictated the first time around, the father is dictating the second time,' Ma said, almost crying, to me.

Ma was not ready for my marriage to Sangita. She preferred a girl from our caste whom my aunt, her sister, had introduced to her. 'Was a Brahmin girl not enough? She has left us with a life of pain. Someone from your own community would never do that. A *biradari* has its own pressure. Who can explain about the *biradari* to outsiders?' Ma swiped away a fly from her nose. She was unhappy about Sangita just as she had been about Vandana. 'Lajwanti was telling me that the girl has done her teachers' training,' Ma said about her sister. 'She will be able to manage the home as well as earn something.'

I was not interested in my marriage…I had no enthusiasm for it but had no objection either. The marriage had to take place, it was happening, and I was a participant. If Ma had won, I would have gone ahead with her. Papa had won and I went ahead with him.

I had met Sangita twice before the wedding. Once at Sudesh chacha's house, and the second time in a large park. I had been quite clear to chacha and my father that her family should be told everything about Vandana. Both had assured me that they had told everything to Sangita and her family. In fact, they had hidden everything. And chachi had conspired with them to do the same.

When we met in the park one evening, I had wanted to tell Sangita everything myself but could not find the right moment. It's also true that I liked Sangita from the start. She was the opposite of Vandana in her seriousness. She had the same philosophy of life as my father—and I liked my father a lot. The most interesting thing was her face. Small-faced Sangita with a large chin, able to say everything with her eyes. She did not need to open her little childlike mouth.

'I had given up on life. You know, don't you, from chacha?' I tried to tell Sangita the truth that evening. In my heart I was afraid that if we went into details, neither of us would be happy, but it was important.

'Yes, yes, but what's happened has happened,' Sangita said. 'You can't stop living your life because of one bad dream.' The subject changed.

'How long have you known chacha?' I asked after a pause.

'Ever since I got admission here,' she said. Then she began to tell me how she had got admission and how, through the Dalit students, she had come to know chachaji. We continued to talk about such things that day.

Then we got married. Sangita's father had arranged a wedding according to Buddhist rituals. Monks read the Panchsheel in Pali. Wedding styles were changing; pandits were replaced by monks. It was a less painful style.

I got a house from the university, and Sangita and I shifted there in the second month. Amma came to live with us straight after the wedding. Sangita was on a month's leave. Amma and Sangita grew very close. When we changed houses, Sangita insisted on bringing Amma with us. One day, Amma let the story of my first marriage escape her, probably when complaining about Vandana.

'I spoke about Vandana to Sangita by mistake, dear,' Amma told me.

I had come home from the university at noon. Sangita had left for her dispensary, which was nearby. She came back after four.

'So what? She knows everything,' I said carelessly while changing my clothes.

'No, she does not know anything. She was asking me every little thing. She was crying, son.' I stopped in my tracks.

'It's possible she didn't know what you were telling her, so she cried. I clearly remember Papa saying he had told her everything.'

'Your Papa told her nothing. He had even forbidden me to tell Sangita anything.' When Amma said this, the earth could have swallowed me up.

I lay down. I was shocked that a truthful and honest person like Papa had told such a huge lie. Could he sacrifice the life of a woman just to see his son happy? Had his attachment to his son overruled other values? I lay there thinking a hundred things, waiting for Sangita. I could not sleep, as I did on other afternoons. Sangita, too, did not come back at 4:30 as on other days. She came at ten minutes past six.

'What happened?' I asked as I opened the door.

I wanted to pretend that nothing had happened, but that was getting impossible. I could not meet her eyes. She did not meet mine. We had spent a proper wedded life of six or seven months together. She did not answer. I closed the door and followed her.

'Are you feeling alright?'

'No,' she said curtly.

'What's happened?'

'Nothing.'

'Say something. Your silence is killing me.'

'Don't you know?' She stood there with the cupboard open, not looking at me.

'But I am not to blame for this,' I said quietly.

'And I am?' she also spoke quietly. I guessed she was crying.

'I was told that you had been told everything. Papa and chacha, both said this. And chachi.'

'Could you…not have told me?'

'I tried, that evening in the park, but you silenced me.'

'I thought you were talking about your inability to join the I.A.S. That's what chachaji told me.' She had still not looked at me.

'I have started loving you, Sangita. I don't know who has told you what lies. I was not part of it. Believe me.'

'If you had had this lie told to you…'

'I am innocent. All this is my father's doing. You should ask him.'

'I am not going to ask anyone anything. I won't be able to live with you.' These were clear words with no shouting or screaming.

'Don't say that. I'll be left alone again. Am I not going to be able to keep any happiness in my life?' I was, as if, asking myself.

'No, it's not possible. I can't.' She had stuffed some clothes in a bag. 'Don't tell Ammaji just now. Tell her after I have left.'

'All right. If you have decided then do as you think right.' I accepted it, though the acceptance was a mistake. Should I have shouted and screamed?

She left. Amma did not come into our room during the conversation. She knew that if a man and a woman cannot resolve their dispute among themselves, then no court or arbitration can resolve it. Nor did she show any reaction on being told of Sangita's departure. I never asked Papa the reason behind all the lies. If you used dishonest means to get your ends, you were not going to get those ends—and so was it in this case.

'Aren't you going to teach today?' Amma came into the room. My face showed the dusty marks of the just-past storm. 'It's been 23 days since Sangita left.' I sighed and thought. When I looked at the clock I realised how the python of time had gobbled me up.

'Yes, I'll go, Amma.'

'What would you like to eat? Should I make an omelette?'

'Whatever you like,' I replied. 'Amma, if you like, you can go to chacha's house. No one will look after you here. Sangita used to do it. Now there is no plan to my going and coming. You will be uncomfortable here and I will worry.'

'You worry about yourself. I am fine. I'll leave when Sangita comes.' Amma's voice had confidence.

'Is she going to come?' My voice was dead.

'She will surely come. My heart tells me. I can't be so wrong in judging a person. She has a large heart. Even a girl from one's own caste can't show such feeling…she's a different kind of girl.' Amma turned away. 'She felt hurt. When she recovers, she will come. I have an open heart for her. My Sangita is a forgiving person.'

Amma left with these blessings.

CHAPTER SIX

Sangita, Gone

I got ready, had breakfast and left for the university. I kept praying the whole way over that somehow Sangita would cross my path. I had been praying in this way for the past 23 days. I would imagine that somewhere on the road, in a restaurant, or the market, I would suddenly meet her. What would she do? Would she refuse to greet me? Would she talk to me? But we never met, though all my pathways were her paths as well.

I kept reading in the library in the afternoon. I ate in the canteen. When I reached home in the evening, I saw that father had come over.

'Papa, when did you come?' I sat beside his chair on the floor.

'I've been here a long time. Do you stay out so late every day? Amma gets worried.' He looked at Amma with anxious eyes.

'Oh no, Panna. He comes early every day. Today I had gone to meet Sangita. He must have thought that he would be alone.' Amma supported me.

'Has Sangita decided to take a divorce for sure, Amma?' Father's voice was dead. 'She is punishing my son for my mistake. Which parent does not want their child's happiness? How is he to blame for what happened?'

'Panna, try to see it from Sangita's side.' Amma told father.

'I cannot see anything in front of my childrens' happiness.' Father looked depressed.

'Leave it. What's happened has happened. We are all right in our own ways, but wrong in others' eyes. What's the cure for that?' I wanted to change the subject. Why court pain and regret? 'Rinku's wedding is fixed,' Amma told me.

'For when?' I asked with pleasure.

'Third April; it's a Friday. It's a holiday, as are the next few days. Guests will find it easy to come.'

'Where are the bride's family from?'

'From our own city. From Sadar Bazaar. The girl is an MBA. She was a student with Rinku, one year junior.'

'They are Suar Khatiks,' Amma said simply. 'Panna got what he wanted. He married all three sons outside the *biradari*.'

'But how are they outside the caste? They are Khatiks, aren't they?' I knew that Amma had put pressure to have the brother after me married within the *biradari*, but Father had had him, too, married outside.

'What is the girl's name?' Amma asked Father.

'Suman Sonkar,' Father replied. 'They are residents of

Allahabad. But Sonkar Sahab was transferred two years ago here to this city. He is a bank manager.'

'The Khatiks, of all in Eastern Uttar Pradesh, have made the most progress. What is his name?'

'Satya Narayan Sonkar…yes, you are right.' Father agreed with me. 'The Khatiks of Rajasthan have not been able to go beyond the burden of their caste. The better they can understand Ambedkar's philosophy, the better will a caste escape their backwardness. The Khatiks of Eastern Uttar Pradesh have understood Ambedkar's thoughts just like the Jatavs of Western Uttar Pradesh.'

'But Panna, these are not Khatiks like us. We have nothing in common—our customs, songs, speech, lifestyle, nothing.' Amma had a question in her voice.

'Amma, you don't know anything. They were also from Rajasthan a long time ago. Their customs changed with their time, as did their clothes, their speech, and so on,' Father explained to Amma. 'Now the Khatiks in Rajasthan are the 'Horse' Khatiks. They also don't intermarry with us. But their customs are the same as ours, their speech and clothing too. Then why not?' Father's voice had become louder.

'You tell me. You have an education. I'm illiterate.' Amma, too, spoke with annoyance.

'Amma, at the time of Islamic rule, many Khatiks had

become Muslims in the Punjab and Sindh region. They were soldiers, not afraid of fighting and killing. The Muslims got stronger with them. The Brahmins calculated that if all the Khatiks were to convert to Islam, their troubles will increase. So, the Rajasthan courts took in the Khatiks. In the Uttar Pradesh and Delhi region, they were given pigs to rear in order to keep them away from Muslims. Muslims find pigs repulsive, that's why. Those who sold dried fruits became the 'Dried fruit-seller' Khatiks; those who worked in the courts became the 'Horse' Khatiks; and those who reared pigs, the 'Pig' Khatiks. They are all actually one.' Father recounted the whole story like the Satyanarayan Katha—the narrative of the god Narayan—as if it were personally witnessed truth.

'Amma, in the proof-of-caste document, only "Khatik" is written,' I agreed with Father.

'Go and explain all this to your mother as well,' Amma said with a laugh.

'No one in the world can make his mother change her ideas. Were you able to, Amma? She has just tolerated me somehow, that's all.'

'Every husband in the world and every wife in the world is unhappy with their spouse. And yet they are making families. This is not short of a miracle, Papa.' I was nursing my own wound.

'In the beginning you don't know much about each other;

and when you do know, a long time together has already passed. The two have become habituated to each other. Then they can only curse each other but cannot leave each other.' Papa had got lost in his memories—maybe of some hurt hidden from us.

Evening was upon us. The dark was throwing a cloak over everything. I got up and turned on the light.

'Why don't you come this way every two or three days, Panna.' Amma drew a quick breath. Because of her breathing problems, she occasionally took such deep breaths.

'Amma, now you just come home with me. Look after the work there. Your daughter-in-law has decided that she will go with the wedding party, tie the turban on her son's head, the lot.' Father's voice was sarcastic.

'That's just fine. Let her fulfill her heart's desire,' Amma said, gesticulating emphatically.

'I was saying the same thing to Amma this morning,' I agreed with Father. 'Who is here to serve her? On the other hand, if I return late, she has to worry about my snacks and meals.'

'Let Sangita come and take over, and I will go back.' Amma took another deep breath.

Father was quiet for some time. Then he cracked his knuckles and said, 'You feel, Amma, that daughter-in-law will come back?'

'I feel that she will come. She has left, but she is still stuck here in her heart.' Amma's face had that same radiance that it had when she talked about dadaji. 'Panna, your Master sahib here is an ass. He doesn't know that Sangita has left home at a time when she needs us the most.' Amma gave a sad smile.

'Why...what's happened?' I asked timidly. Amma had made the atmosphere mysterious.

'Panna, I am going to become a great-grandmother.' I felt a tickle inside me on hearing Amma's words. 'She told me today. I had gone to meet her. But she was talking of an abortion.' Amma was speaking without feeling.

I wished with all my heart that I could somehow reach Sangita. I would touch her feet, ask forgiveness for the crime I had not committed, but how could she kill our child? It wasn't our child. It was our dream. The magic that would make my 10 years of suffering disappear. The meaning of our existence, for both Sangita and me.

'I'll try to talk to them again,' said Father. 'I'll ask Sudesh and Sukhjot to talk to them.'

'Who will have the courage to talk to her? Truth and justice are on her side.' Amma voiced defeat.

'We want to correct our mistake,' Father explained. 'She will surely give us another chance. What did you talk to her about?'

'I asked her finally if Masterji was to blame for anything,' Amma said looking at me.

'And what did she say,' I asked.

'Nothing. She just started crying.'

'Fine, let me see.' Father got up with an effort. 'If you can come a few days early for the wedding, I'll have some support,' he told me.

'Yes, sir. I'll keep coming by.' Amma's words had filled me with sadness.

Father left. Amma and I kept sitting. We kept sitting quietly for a long time. I had nothing to say and nothing to ask. Amma's news had increased my confusion. I was a father! I wanted to laugh, to cry, to dance. However, I kept sitting quietly.

'Should I ask Sangita to come to the wedding?'

'Yes, ask her. At least you'll be able to talk to her.' Amma's voice lacked enthusiasm.

'Where is she living?'

'Some place near the dispensary.'

'A house or a hostel?'

'A hostel, I think. It didn't look like a house to me.'

'I'll talk to her on her mobile phone.' I went around the room many times, then sat down.

'Go ahead, child,' Amma caressed my head. 'Don't lose Sangita. Don't be proud.'

'I know, Amma, but tell me…what can I do? Where can I go? Who can I tell about my problem?'

'Don't worry. I know that you are innocent. Sangita can't stay away no matter what. If your heart is pure, you will win.

She will come back sooner or later. Put yourself in her position. If this had been done by Sangita and you had no knowledge of it, how would you react? That's what is happening with Sangita. Your heart should know what is good or bad for yourself. You have to switch places to know another's pain and happiness. Your reflection is in her soul. If she does not come back to you, she will not go to anyone else either. My old eyes have seen the world. I have seen the glow of auspiciousness on her forehead…I have seen nectar in her eyes…after all these years…my tired old eyes…' Amma kept muttering. She was somewhere else, and the person caressing my head was someone else. 'If truthfulness is not for show, it can colour everything. A truthful person may suffer but does not feel pain. There is great power in truth.'

I had thought of Ayesha when I heard this. I thought of Kalra and Firoz. They were false and dishonest in the eyes of the world but not in their own eyes. They had only tried to see the world with their own eyes. Is it a crime to live according to your own view of the world? And if it is, then we are all criminals. I, Ayesha, Kalra, Firoz—everyone. Sangita and Amma too, and Father as well.

'What should I cook?' I asked Amma. The clock was showing eight.

'Anything at all.' Amma did not turn around. 'There's a pumpkin in the kitchen.'

I knew that Amma did not eat potatoes. I did not like

pumpkin. To make a potato curry would have seemed the best thing at the moment.

I loved the potato-mustard chokha made by Vandana, a Bihari chokha aromatic with mustard oil, that I never tasted after Vandana left. It reminded me of her. One time she was making chokha in the kitchen and I was playing around with her. She kept trying to stop me and I would not stop. Finally, she had emptied the bowl full of mustard oil on my head.

'There. I've made your chokha.' She kept laughing. I picked her up by the waist and threw her on the bed.

'What did you eat?' Vandana's eyes were mischievous as she traced the hair on my chest with her fingers half an hour later, drenched with sweat.

With Vandana, the taste of potato chokha as well as the sweetness of mustard oil had departed.

When I entered the kitchen to cook the pumpkin for Amma, I saw that she had already peeled, chopped and washed it. 'Amma, really,' I thought to myself. I put refined oil in the pressure cooker and put it on the fire. While the oil heated, I cut some onions and cleaned some cumin seeds. I fried the vegetable with the onion, cumin, some turmeric and salt. My hand went to the chili powder but I remembered Amma and left it. She did not like her *gheeya* to be hot. I would have a green chili on the side at such times.

The fuss that I created about food as a child changed to the exact opposite as an adult. Especially after Vandana's departure and my stay in prison. The amount of salt in a vegetable, whether there was chili or not, were not grounds for complaint. One day Mother served mutton, and I kept eating it absent-mindedly. When Rinku sat down to eat, he announced that there was no salt in it. Mother first told off Meena, my younger brother Chiku's wife who had made the mutton, then she looked at me and kept crying, 'Son, what's happened to you?'

While the cooker gave its first whistle, I mixed the flour for Amma's roti. If I put ghee in the flour for her, the roti would be soft. She could chew it easily. She dipped it in the juice of the vegetable and ate.

'Move over,' came Amma's voice. I was now mixing the flour for myself. 'Give it to me, let me do it.'

'Yours is done,' I said, continuing.

'Why did you do it, I'd do it.' She usually made her rotis herself.

'I just did the two together.'

'Did you put the momin or forget?' Amma called the ghee in the flour momin instead of moyen.

'I put it, I put it.' I laughed. 'Having a feast on the ghee in our old age, aren't we?'

'Well, if my children are feeding me, I'm feasting away.' Amma laughed as well. 'In my youth your grandfather fed me ghee, now I am having it at your place. After his death, it was a job to run the household, where would I get ghee?' At 76 or 77, Amma still did not leave her work for anyone. From washing her clothes to making her rotis, she did all her work herself.

Amma left for a walk after dinner and asked me to come along. Usually, we went together. But I refused because I had to make some phone calls. I phoned Ayesha, Kalra, Rana, Aslam, Vedprakash, Sushil, Firoz, Jayant and Sangita, as well as some other special people. Jayant, now an Indian Police Service officer, was posted in Nahan in Himachal Pradesh.

Sushil was working in our city as a DCP. He had done a lot for the city. He had either had the violent criminals killed off or put behind bars, but he was not talked about in the newspapers proportionate to his work. Sushil belonged to the Gujarat cadre but upon the pull of a Dalit Cabinet Minister Bhardashil Jatia, he was posted in our city.

'Why, you were the one who claimed that Jatav caste members would never do anything for other Dalits,' I asked him one day on the phone.

'I was wrong,' Sushil said without hesitation. 'When the Minister heard about my mother's illness, he did my work in a week. The Jatavs are the Dalits' saviours.'

'And will the Brahmins help others at all?'

'They also have some good people among them… Not all…'

I laughed. 'Which caste has all good people or all bad?'

'I am not going to comment on that.' Sushil was now a member of the country's highest service cadre and showed professional tact.

'Life is a journey, Sushil. We have to cover it separately and alone. We can be on different stopping points along it. We are not on different journeys. Life is a battle for power. The sooner we accept that, the sooner we will have peace. From the Buddha to Ambedkar, everyone has ripened to this knowledge.'

'So should we give up our struggle? You say some absurd things sometimes, pal.' There was some heat in his voice.

'When did I say this? I merely said that only after comprehending this power struggle can we have peace. Too much emotion makes us angry and violent. We should fight, but deliberately. Violence is not deliberate. At the most it could be a strategy, but a strategy must be made deliberately, not emotionally.'

'But our fight is not about power, it's about truth.' Sushil's voice was full of tension.

'I agree with you.' I had some questions, however.

Could not this fight for truth be considered the first step of the fight for power? If it was a fight for truth for the group, was it not a fight for power for the individual? And if indeed these first steps had nothing to do with power, then why were non-Dalits so determined to end a fight simply for Truth?

'This is a contempt they have harboured for centuries. Brahmins do not want that our communities should rise up. They hate us. Their hearts are full of live coals.' Sushil was boiling over.

I stayed silent. I was wondering if any caste at all loved another caste? Not just Dalits, Brahmins did not want any other caste to rise up. From Vashisht and Vishwamitra, Parashuram and Sahastrarjun, to Ilachandra Joshi and Premchandra Srivastava, this was an obvious fact. Hindi novelist and short story writer Ilachandra Joshi's 'Joshi' and the king of storytelling Premchand's hidden, implicit 'Srivastava' had drawn my attention. They were their caste marks.

Did not the conflict extend to Brahmins among themselves, and Chamar with Chamar? Did other high castes or other backward castes want other castes to rise up? Did Jats, or Gujars, or Yadavs, or Kurmis and Koiries, Reddys and Marathas?

'You have a special love for Brahmins.' Sushil could not keep silent upon seeing me silent. 'That same weakness showed itself in your marriage to Vandana.' He made a personal attack. He was unable to understand me even now.

'I have a special love for human beings. I may be wrong, but I take responsibility for my thoughts. Nothing is final, and neither are these thoughts. Who knows, I may start thinking like you tomorrow, but today, at this instance, till this breath, this is what I think, and with full honesty. Who knows about tomorrow?'

I deliberately did not respond to his personal attack. Maybe I thought that those who work in the social sphere do not have any personal causes anymore. If I wanted, I could have asked him some personal questions too—such as how, in one year, he had earned such wealth when Jayant was still in the same condition as before? Why did he not dedicate his whole life to a single cause like Jayant? Was the addiction to airconditioned homes and cars, expensive liquor and perfumed women also a part of his struggle for truth? These questions would have only increased bitterness and distance.

I could not forget that Sushil was not just my friend any longer; he was a high-ranking police officer. Sometimes it is not the greed for profit but the fear of loss that makes us tactful.

Ayesha was very pleased to get the invitation to Rinku's wedding. I was afraid of my secrets coming out, but they had to come out some day or the other. This was the right time. I did think that Kalra must have told Ayesha about my marriage and my family, but I was wrong. He had not told her anything. This was made evident only when she came to my house. She was very enthusiastic about joining in, in my family celebrations.

'Can I come a couple of days before the wedding?' she had asked.

'Whatever for? There are only some family rituals before that.'

'I want to be part of a family. I want to see what a family is like. What brother and sister, mother and father, uncles and aunts, sisters-in law and brothers-in-law are like. I want to see what is the magic that binds them all together. You will have some trouble, but please do it for me, Masterji,' Ayesha had asked on the phone.

I wanted to see her face as she said this. I had this strange obsession.

When I had finished talking to everyone else, I had called Sangita on her mobile.

'Rinku's wedding is on the third.' I was unable to say her name and blurted this out as soon as she said hello.

She was quiet for some time. A few days apart had put up some barriers between us.

'Papaji phoned me, just a while ago,' she said softly.

'How are you?' I gathered courage and asked.

'...' There was no reply from the other side.

'Are you well?' I asked the silence on the other side.

'How are you?' her voice came after a few minutes.

Those minutes were longer than my life.

'How can I live without you?' I was actually very moved.

'All this is useless now.' Sangita's voice seemed very unfamiliar.

'Why?'

'That's how things are,' she said after much thought.

'Everything is out and open before you now,' I said pleadingly.

'Who knows? Lying and cheating only comes out in installments.'

'You are being unfair.' A hardness came into my voice. I forgot Amma's advice.

'More unfair than you?' Her voice trembled.

'Do you want a divorce? It's your decision.' Against my will, I became harder still.

'Yes.' She spoke with decisiveness and ignored the hardness in my voice.

'Will we be enemies if we are not husband and wife?' I retrieved my balance. Was I also playing games like Vandana?

She was quiet on hearing this. I could guess what was going on in her mind. She was a very straightforward woman.

'I will come on the third, just for a short while. You will not try to talk to me. I am coming just for Ammaji.' She tried to remove any misunderstanding.

'I promise.' At this point I wanted to protect myself. Was I behaving towards Sangita as Vandana used to towards me?

CHAPTER SEVEN

Towards the Wedding

Ayesha arrived on the 31st of March. I had asked Father to reserve one floor upstairs for my guests. Ayesha stayed there; I was expecting more later.

On the 1st began the *haldi* and *tel* rituals on Rinku. He was going to be scrubbed with turmeric and oil many times over—seven times in three days to be precise. The ritual was also called '*ban baithna*' or 'setting up the shine', and could go on for three-to-five days, but the number of turmeric massages had to be seven. The wedding was on the third. There could not be a turmeric scrub the same day. So, Rinku had no option but to subject himself to three or four turmeric massages the day before.

People make rituals and then find themselves prisoners within them.

My buas, father's sisters, had come. Close cousins and their wives had come. Everyone had conspired to make a mess of Rinku with the turmeric. Ayesha had also done the ritual.

She had become one of the family from the first day. All the women were curious about her. Mother told them that she worked with Sangita. Mother, the aunts and the cousins all completed rituals one by one while Amma sat by and directed them. Mother was annoyed. 'Amma, leave these; they are really old rites.' She kept being annoyed by, and also completing, every last ritual.

Ayesha was beaming with pleasure during all this.

Sangita arrived on the day of the wedding—she had already made it clear to me that she would come only on that day.

The house was bustling with guests when she reached; I had just returned with the milk. It happened that I was the first person she saw. I went up to her but she hurriedly entered and stood next to Rinku. Rinku, on seeing her, stood up.

'Bhabhi, namaste.' He touched Sangita's feet. 'It's so good you are here.' Sangita stopped him from touching her feet.

Rinku was seven or eight years younger than me. In the five days of turmeric massages, his fair skin had started shining like gold. He and I both resembled Father, but he was fair like Mother whereas I was dark like Papa. Chiku had both my mother's looks and her complexion.

Sangita stepped forward and touched Amma's and Mother's feet, then bua's, who was nearby. I could see from the back that Sangita had lost weight.

'Sangita, why, you are great. We do the turmeric and oil rituals for your brother-in-law and you stay at your job.' My older aunt laughed.

'Why, she sent her friend to look after the work here.' The younger aunt said to the older one. There was a mystery in her way of saying this, and a tension.

'Your friend is upstairs. Go and meet her,' Ma told Sangita, looking at me.

Sangita's face showed uncertainty.

'Come,' I said, and Sangita turned to look at me with sharp questions in her eyes. But she did not ask anything, just followed me silently upstairs.

Just then, Chiku and his wife Meena came out of their room and also touched Sangita's feet. Their faces were lit with pleasure.

Were they all sad with me in my sorrow? Did they also wish with me that there would be a permanent flow of happy moments in my life? Could anyone at all expect any permanence in happiness—or unhappiness?

I was overcome with emotion when Meena said to Sangita, 'It will be total injustice, didi, that we have made you into an aunt and you are not going to give us that pleasure.' Sangita smiled and stroked Meena's head.

'Your didi is not as fortunate as you, Meena.' Father must have given the news of Sangita's pregnancy to Mother, who must have told Meena. Probably what Sangita was saying about fortune was just a figure of speech.

'You are looking thin,' I whispered to her as we climbed upstairs. She did not reply. I repeated what I had said and she remained silent. I was trying, but my words had no meaning.

We were, all of us, in the wrong—myself, Papa, Mummy, Amma, Uncle. We could move forward only with acceptance of this and with abject humility. It was up to Sangita to forgive us. She was the victim, she was in the right, so she was superior to us. Wasn't it the same situation as of Dalits with Brahmins, people of colour with Whites, women with men? I seemed to have a hang-up to see everything through this lens of hierarchy.

We reached Ayesha's door. I knocked.

'Oh, Masterji, it's you. The door was open. I had not locked it from inside, just closed it hard.' Ayesha's eyes fell on Sangita. 'I was taking a bath.' She put the orange towel she had on her head on her shoulders.

'Ayesha, this is Sangita, my wife.' I spoke entering the room, pulling Ayesha in. Sangita followed.

'Sangita, this is Ayesha, my friend. She was interested in observing the whole wedding celebration. Ma decided to introduce her to everyone as your friend. Ayesha, she did not know you at all, so it was important for her to meet you. Some relatives are very conservative.' I introduced Ayesha and Sangita to each other.

Ayesha's face had fallen. This was an unforeseen turn of events for her. Sangita's face was tense. She was not the same as she had been just moments ago with Mother and Amma. Was my tactic working?

Whatever Ayesha's past had been, no one could look at her without being charmed. Sangita was also attractive, but faded before Ayesha's unmatched beauty. Ayesha's fair complexion glowed after her bath. Bua had put turmeric on her cheeks in the morning. With her damp hair and blushing colour, she looked the very picture of innocence.

'Sit, didi.' Ayesha established a convenient sisterly relation with Sangita.

'What do you do?' Sangita woke up after a pause.

'I...' Ayesha looked at me.

'Ayesha is a social worker. She works with an NGO. We met during a camp.' I lied again.

Was Sangita correct that lies don't get revealed all at once? But this did not seem the time to tell the truth. We are mortals after all.

'What do you do didi?' Ayesha was collecting herself.

'Didn't he tell you?' Sangita's voice had a hint of harshness, contrary to my hopes.

'Masterji did not even tell me about your marriage.' Ayesha smiled.

'So, he would hardly have told you about his earlier marriage?'

Sangita's anger was coming out. I had found the right spot. If she did not express her anger, it would fester into a deep wound. Ayesha was the most appropriate weapon for this.

Was I hurting both Sangita and Ayesha with my cleverness? I had asked myself that question and knew the answer. I really wanted their well-being. Of course, I wanted my own, but for that I was not hurting them at all. Indeed, they could hurt themselves far more with their own feelings, which in turn would have hurt me also. In saving myself, I hoped I was saving them too.

My only aim, for myself and for them, was to live a life of peace. My aim was certainly not to injure them in any way. My conscience was clear that this cleverness was not an injury, but rather an honest and careful attempt to save their and my futures.

'There is no place for these things in Ayesha and my relationship.' I tried to say this simply as a factual, not ironical, statement. 'We both know our limits. We do not consider friendship "unauthorized encroachment"; we try to be careful of each other's personal space.'

And, in fact, whenever Ayesha seemed reluctant to answer a question, I never asked her again. I was not even aware of when Ayesha, such a close friend now, did not tell me something. Why should we not respect each other's independence and comfort? Was our past, either Ayesha's or mine, proving an obstacle in our lives in the present? Then why go poking into it? If the past did not give us strength and energy, and make our present beautiful and productive, why did we have to clutch it to our breasts like a monkey her dead baby? Its decaying smell would ruin the present also.

'That is absolutely correct, Masterji. Most married couples, instead of living in the present, kill themselves trying to find out each other's love affairs before marriage. Where is the deep, closed well that does not also have some fresh air blowing through it…' Ayesha's words had helped my strategy, though she had spoken without knowing it.

'You are very beautiful, Ayesha…you look exactly like Marilyn Monroe.' Either Sangita had deliberately changed the subject or she was annoyed by Ayesha's beauty.

Girls or women of the same age don't usually complement each other on their beauty. Was this some strategy of Sangita's?

'You are also very beautiful, didi.' Ayesha's eyes were shining, partly for Sangita and partly, perhaps, for me.

'Nothing in comparison to you. Your Masterji must be pleased with you.' Sangita dug in a little.

'If a man is complete and satisfied in body and mind in his own home, he won't look outside for his pleasures.' Ayesha had been quiet for a minute after Sangita's barb. Her words after the pause unsettled Sangita.

'He is like a god. He could commit a mistake, but not a sin.'

When a prostitute voluntarily, without an explicit or implicit pressure from anyone, gives a certificate of virtue to a man or woman, then it is truly remarkable.

'I'll be going.'

Sangita was going towards the door as if she could not take it anymore. I also got up with Sangita.

'You wait,' Ayesha said to me. Sangita stopped and looked at me.

I was also looking at her. My eyes were asking for some understanding, or maybe had a question.

'Please come downstairs. I have some work.' Sangita told me directly. She did not wait but left through the door.

'You get ready and come downstairs, Ayesha.' I deliberately waited a bit inside and then left.

Sangita was waiting near the door. She had not gone down the stairs yet. I silently thanked Ayesha. When she saw me coming, Sangita moved towards the stairs, very slowly. She moved so slowly only when she was in a mental turmoil. When she was angry, she would become totally silent. She was silent now. I also did not speak as we descended the stairs. She went straight to Amma who was sitting in the courtyard. Before she could reach Amma, Chhoti bua caught her.

'Put some turmeric on Rinku with your own hands,' she said.

'Buaji, that woman is not a friend of mine.' Sangita told bua in a clear, deep voice.

'Yes, yes, we know. If your mother-in-law does not tell us, won't we find out ourselves?' Bua said softly, like someone unveiling a mystery. Meanwhile, I had appeared from behind the stairs.

'She is his friend.'

'So what?' Bua came up to me and caught my arm as soon as she saw me. 'These friendships and so on are all fine in educated households. There is no caste-community here to gossip. Had there been, this would have been talked about far and wide.' Bua paused. 'There are some advantages and some disadvantages of being educated.'

'I won't stop you from anything,' I said to Sangita. 'They all know, but they will all stand by me. They will like or dislike me but won't give me up. I've lived in the community, Sangita. It'll be difficult for you to understand its nature. The caste and the community have a special nature. You should, of course, do what you think fit.'

Sangita seemed lost in thought as she stood there hitting the ground with her sandal's heel.

'You are truly a masquerader. A traveller from port to port.' Maybe she wanted to hurt me with her words. This would make her feel better. Bua's response must have deflated her.

'This is just how human beings are, Sangita.' I hung my head and agreed softly with her so that she could indeed have the satisfaction of victory.

She went and sat at Amma's feet. I stood there watching her. Amma was lying on the diwan and she started massaging Amma's feet. She might have been the one to suggest that Amma lie down—I couldn't hear from afar. They were talking among themselves.

I pulled a chair and sat down. On their left, Rinku was sleeping on a mat on the ground.

Last night had been an all-night watch for the ancestors. The men had stayed up playing cards and had fallen asleep, exhausted, by two or three. The women had stayed up all night, including Ayesha. They had sung songs for the ancestors all night.

In the morning when I was leaving for milk, Ayesha came up to me humming. 'I have learnt many of the songs. Go and bring the milk and I'll sing them for you.' Maybe she had tried to detain me upstairs for that.

I fell asleep in my chair with these thoughts. When the noise awoke me, the scene had changed. Rinku was on a low stool, being ritually massaged with oil. The younger bua, older bua, Meena and two female cousins from the village were all engrossed in that. Amma was not on the diwan.

Had Sangita left? I got up with a start.

'Bua, where is Amma?' I asked bua.

'Hey, Pushpa, where is sister-in-law?' Bua asked her older sister.

'Amma, Amma,' I shouted.

'Amma is in the front room...why are you shouting?' asked the older bua.

I went to the room. Amma was resting, but Sangita was not there. 'Amma!' I called out softly, but she did not hear me through her sleep. The outer wall was bathed in sunshine from the window. Maybe that was why Amma had decided to come and sleep here.

So where was Sangita? With Ayesha...I ran to the stairs and upstairs. Ayesha's laughter filled the terrace.

I ran all the way to the room. The door was open. Before I could see Ayesha's face, I saw Sangita's back.

'Come...please come.' Ayesha stood up.

'I thought...you had left.' I was panting.

'That was what you wanted.' Sangita's face held a combination of disappointment, indifference and sarcasm.

'I want that you never leave.' Sangita's face came to life at this.

Is this what she wanted to hear in front of Ayesha?

'Alright, Masterji, should I sing one of the nighttime songs for you?' Ayesha spoke up restlessly like a child.

Did she want it to seem that there was nothing between Sangita and me?

'Rinku is getting the haldi ritual. Do it also.' My request to Sangita had a trace of emotional blackmail—why was I doing that?'

'Didi can do it in the evening. It will happen again. There's a total of seven haldis and this is only the sixth. Why don't you listen to how I've learnt this song.' Ayesha was chirruping again. 'Just tell me if you want to hear the haldi song or the nighttime song. And you have to explain the meaning too. I only memorised it.'

'Sing us the nighttime song.' Sangita turned down my request and responded to Ayesha instead.

In spite of this rebuff, I did not feel insulted. I sat down on the bed too. Ayesha started without any preface or hesitation. She sang the ancestors song verbatim.

'I could not understand anything, Ayesha.' Sangita gestured her ignorance. She also made a face, as if she was unable to understand anything.

'I understand it...' Ayesha moved both her hands in reassurance. 'The ancestors, that is the dead relatives, of the boy getting married are being made to feel in this song that they are included. He is sleeping in his cot, which the grandfather, the grandmother, the uncle, the aunt, push in turn to swing, and this cot is especially made by a carpenter out of fragrant sandalwood.

'Who explained this to you?' I asked because I myself did not know the meaning of the words.

'I'm Bengali. I know magic.' She laughed loudly. 'No, no, Ammaji told me.'

I had never seen Ayesha laugh so much. Was the laughter some kind of cover? She was speaking fast and not giving anyone else a chance to speak. 'Should I sing one more, didi?'

'Yes, sing.' Sangita's voice was enthusiastic.

Was it the magic of music, or the desire to show indifference to me, or to pull Ayesha to her side as much as possible?

Then there was Ayesha, who was getting so excited that she started the minute Sangita said yes. There could be no doubt she had a beautiful voice. She sang another song in full.

All around the well, poppy seeds have been planted,
And decorative henna has been planted
Stay here, old grandfather
Stay here, old grandfather
This is your city.
The opium will be drunk by dear grandfather
The opium will be drunk by dear grandfather
The henna will be applied by dearest grandmother
Oh, please stay here, my old fathers
This is your city.

'I can understand this song a bit.' Sangita snapped her fingers. 'Posat means posto or opium.' Sangita looked at me. 'If I am not mistaken.'

'You are right.' I wanted to catch Sangita's hand that had advanced in my direction. 'Isn't there a similar song in Punjabi in your place, where all the relatives are paraded one by one?' I had asked a question but Sangita kept quiet.

'How?' Ayesha jumped in. She was in a strange mood.

'I don't know a whole lot. For instance…"I worked for 12 years, and after all that labour, got myself a bride. But the wedding can only work if my father dances at it. The wedding will be colourful only if my father dances"…'

I had just recited the song without tune or rhythm.

'Didi, please sing it for us.' Ayesha clapped and shouted. 'Masterji has ruined it completely.

'Another time. I must go downstairs now. I have to go in the evening so I should do the haldi now.' Sangita started getting up. 'We can do that much for friends.' She looked at me. Maybe her praise in front of Ayesha had made a space for me in her heart.

'You'll go only if I let you go!' Ayesha got up as well.

I got up too, seeing them both on their feet. I would have liked for us to keep talking like this till the end of time. Ayesha's delighted chirpiness and Sangita's calmness felt very nice to me. I wanted to keep looking at Sangita. We came down.

As bua did haldi, she sang the same song that Ayesha had sung coming down the stairs.

'Listen, didi! They are singing the same song!' Ayesha said excitedly. She looked at me and started humming alongside.

My son's hair is English-style
Always use a comb.
He is the star of my eyes.
Never make him cry.

The boy's grandfather said,
He is the star of my eyes,
Never make him cry.
His hair is English-style
Always use a comb.

The boy's grandmother said,
He is the star of my eyes,
Never make him cry.

The boy's mother said…

Ayesha had rejoined the group of singing women. Meena gave her and Sangita haldi, and they were putting it on Rinku. Ayesha was singing with the women in an exceptionally high voice, almost in an aggressively rural way. Sangita only kept smiling and putting haldi.

I had started pondering on the social dimensions of the song. Did the bridegroom's locks being English-style call for a comb? Did villagers not keep a comb otherwise? Was this imitation of British ways not an imitation of the upper classes, 'Sanskritisation,' as it is called?

Don't pluck the unripe fruit
O man from the city
The plant will die.

Bua had started a new song in a loud voice. There was a new laugh on the women's faces. Sangita was also laughing. Did she understand the meaning?

Lata's voice was the sharpest and earthiest. Ayesha's voice was the most tuneful. Sangita's voice could not be heard at all, but she had become part of the group.

Did this prove that an action originally performed with deliberate effort gradually becomes normal behaviour?

Bua had started a new song.

Stones in the well
Only half-full of water
Don't be so helpless

Pull! Pull!
Pull! Pull!
Take a silken cord
From the bhabhi's pyjamas
Bridegroom!

Ayesha was laughing. Sangita was smiling, and so was Meena. Lata was giggling; she was not singing. Only the aunts were singing. They were keeping time on Meena and Sangita's shoulders.

'Oh…girls, what is all this, stop it.' Amma shouted out.

Bua kept singing.

'Pushpa, be quiet.' Amma came and stood there. Seeing her, Pushpa bua brought her singing to a halt.

Oh, there is a bazaar behind the pump
My bridegroom went there for fun.

Amma started singing and all the women said, 'Oh yes!' and joined in the song.

Dada ji is searching in the lanes around
Dada ji is searching in the lanes around
Dadi is calling out
My bridegroom has gone out to play.

Lata took the song forward in a strong voice:

> *Tauji is searching in the lanes around…*

Chhoti bua was not one to wait. She continued:

> *Oh dear, the bazaar is behind our courtyard*
> *My bridegroom set out to play,*
> *Uncle is searching in the lanes around…*

To my surprise, Ayesha also carried the song forward:

> *Brother is searching in the lanes around…*

'Well, kid, you are learning fast! Our cat's meow is louder than ours!' Bua's aiming this at Ayesha made everyone laugh.

Ayesha looked shyly at me, which Sangita saw. Her face became tense.

Now, do women have a sixth sense to spot every look, or was it love?

'Buaji, I can sing that other song with any name in it that you like,' Ayesha said enthusiastically.

'Don't get into these songs Ayesha,' said Amma. 'This is only for uneducated people, using songs to mouth abuses.'

'Well, well. Look at our Lady, the Bridegroom's Mother.' Bari bua gave Amma a hug. 'My sweet old mother, her Ladyship, the Bridegroom's Mother,' bua sang out the last part.

As they finished up the haldi ritual, they kept singing the same songs in different combinations. Mother didn't have a moment's rest. She would go out for something, or pause near the singers, or go into a room to find something, or pull a stool just anywhere to sit. She was happy. All this went on till 12:30 pm.

'When will your brothers come?' Father asked Mother, his voice angry. 'We had said 10 in the morning and it's 3 already.'

'3? It's only 12,' Mother answered.

'Well, do you plan to make it 3?' Father hit back. 'When will I take the barat procession to the bride's house?'

'They must be on their way. Why should they come so early and just sit here? They may not be free.' Mother said. 'There's always work to be done.'

'It will get late. Be warned.'

'Is everyone here from your side?' said Mother sarcastically. 'Chiku, phone your uncles and find out when they'll be here.

'They've left,' said Chiku. 'I just talked to them.'

'I hope you heard that,' Mother said testily.

'Yes, I heard it fine,' Father said, leaving. 'I've been hearing it and suffering it for 35 years.'

'Is there a quarrel about something?' Ayesha asked, pulling up a chair next to me.

'No, nothing. They talk angrily like this at any special occasion. They are not quarrelling,' I clarified.

The tent house boys had brought in a basket of snacks. I took some on a plate and a jug of tea, and climbed up to Ayesha's room. Ayesha followed me. I looked back at Sangita, who was sitting next to Amma and watching us. But she kept watching and didn't budge.

CHAPTER EIGHT

The Bhat, the Ritual Lunch

When I came downstairs at around 2:30, all three aunts—my mamis, or mother's brothers' wives—were sitting next to Amma. Ayesha was in her room; I had taken a nap in the next room. I greeted the three aunts.

'Has Sangita left?' I asked Amma.

'Your wife…yes, she was leaving just as we reached.' Chhoti mami, the youngest aunt, replied before Amma could.

All three aunts were weighed down with ornaments, but the youngest, Chhoti mami, looked like a walking-talking jewellery shop.

'Didi, is daughter-in-law a Punjabi?' Middle mami asked the oldest one.

'No, didi, she is supposed to be a Chamar.' Chhoti mami was the one to butt in again.

Her husband, my Chhote mama or youngest uncle, had a fruit business that had started running well. My mami's tongue had started running as well. Chhoti mami was from

Jaipur. I had heard from childhood that women from Jaipur were big talkers.

'No, no,' middle mami corrected her, maybe to thicken the plot.

'Well, she's certainly pretty. Fair and smooth-skinned. She's a doctor,' the older mami added.

'Here is baiji. Let's ask her,' said the invincible Chhoti mami.

'What do you want to know?' asked Mother.

'Bhabhi, she is calling your oldest daughter-in-law a Chamar.'

'And so what?' Bari bua appeared and attacked. 'It's Brahmins who have made up castes and sub-castes. Everyone leaves God's house the same.'

'So, am I saying anything bad?' Chhoti mami was impossible to silence. 'Baiji has put together quite a clan: one daughter-in-law a Chamar, one a Koli and one, a Suar Khatik,' she placed her bid.

'So, should we have brought a 10th fail from Jaipur into the clan?' Bari bua outbid her.

Chhoti mami was from Jaipur and was 10th fail. She was, of course, insulted. It didn't help that her two sisters-in-law, the oldest and the middle mamis, laughed out aloud.

Chhoti mami was shocked at the treachery by the oldest and middle mamis at the moment she needed them. Who knows but the other two had a built-up annoyance against her, for which they had taken revenge at the right moment? What a great battle these family exchanges always are. Mother was full of gratitude for bua who had acted as her shield at the moment of attack. Bua was an expert at this warfare. Her neighbourhood in the city was full of caste members. Even a child in that place would know how to give an appropriate reply. The caste-community gave a silent, powerful education.

'Please sit in the tent, all of you, and let's start lunch,' Amma said. She asked bua to call Father. She knew that if she sat with them, the talk would continue.

Father came. He told Amma to start the *bhat*, the ritual community lunch. I had Ayesha sent for. We all went and stood in the tent. The guests in the tent were divided into two. On one side were people from Mother's natal family, including the three mamis and their children. On the other side were people from our paternal clan.

Mother was standing between the two sides with her face veiled. Chhote mama, her younger brother, was gifting her new saris—each more expensive and lovely than the other. Bua was taking them from her and putting them on one side. A respectable elder from the community was calling out the names of those who had gifted the saris. 'This is from Ramgarh's Hari Khinchi, this is from Lakshmangarh's Babulal Sawanriya, this is from the bride's uncles…' he was calling out.

All through my childhood I had heard such a call-out on the occasion of weddings and bhat lunches. A woman started a bhat song, in which the woman's natal family was asked to make sure to give a proper gift to her father-in-law, mother-in-law, brother-in-law and everyone else.

O residents of Lakshmanpur,
Bring proper bhat gifts....

Bring my father-in-law a turban
A green turban

Bring my mother-in-law a shawl
A shawl inlaid with gems

Bring your brother-in-law a suit
Make him a sahib with suit and boots

And bring your sister-in-law a sari
Make her a memsahib with a sari

Ayesha was standing near me.

'Were Mother's ancestors from Lakshmangarh?' she asked.

'Yes, you guessed right.'

Ayesha was pleased at that.

A different song started from another side.

Let us give an invitation to bhat
To the people of Lakshmangarh
And on the pretext of an invitation
See my father
I was born and my mother
Became sterile after that

There was pain in the words 'my mother became sterile', and the singers' voices were full of pain.

I have neither a nephew
Nor any other male relative
My father is a yogi
Unable to give bhat gifts…
Let us go to Lakshmangarh
And on the pretext of an invitation
See how my father is doing.

The voices of the singers were drowned in pain. I heard a sob near me and turned to see Ayesha crying profusely.

In reply to the question in my eyes, she said, 'I am such an unfortunate person, Masterji. I have no one in the world.'

I was silent.

Mother, standing in the middle of the relatives, had sat down on her haunches right there and was crying. Bua was trying to raise her, but maybe she just couldn't get up. Then her two brothers, the older and middle mama, came and sat down on their haunches besides her. Bare mama, older uncle, was caressing her head lovingly. This made her cry louder. Bare mama became tearful as well. The women's singing had stopped.

'Don't be silly, sister. Don't cry,' bare mama said with a catch. 'We are here.' All three brothers embraced her.

'Oh, brother, my father!' Mother let out a cry for her father.

At which the three mamas all burst into tears. The whole atmosphere was transformed. Ayesha was crying here near me. Mother and the mamas were wailing there. All the voices in the tent had stopped. The only sounds were their crying, Ayesha's sobs, and the sound of the pedestal fan.

Just then a woman's voice from Mother's natal family arose in song. I recognised it as Chhoti mami's voice.

My sister-in-law used her wiles
To win over her brother
To win over her brother
My sister-in-law with her wiles
Won over her brother
He sold off my armlet

Is going to sell my bracelet
He will give his sister all the gifts
And leave me naked
Oh, she has used her wiles
To entrap her brother.

Chhoti mami's single voice was joined in a few seconds by the older and middle mamis' voices, then by some other women's. Mama had started laughing. Mother was perhaps smiling as well inside her veil. Everyone was restored to their previous selves, and were talking and singing. Only Ayesha remained like a ghost.

The voices kept singing, verse after verse.

He has sold off my waistband…
He will give his sister all the gifts
And leave me naked.
Oh, she has used her wiles
To entrap her brother.

Is this what it is, the family's magnetism and its power? Is this what Ayesha is crying for? Is this what saves us from the world's biggest suffering, loneliness? The mamis kept singing. Their one song had blown away the dark clouds that had gathered.

The bhat continued. After Mother, Father was given clothes and gifts. Then Chiku and I, and our wives, were given clothes as well. They had brought a warm suit and a sherwani for Rinku. The sherwani was for the wedding, and the suit for colder weather. They had brought him a thick gold chain and gold ring as well.

After the gifts, lunch began.

CHAPTER NINE

Ayesha's Style

In the evening everybody was getting the bridegroom's procession, the *barat*, ready. The horse and the band were already at the door; the band was playing. Everyone was trying to hurry. It was already six and there was no sign of Sangita. Rinku was being dressed up and the older brother-in-law, jija, was his helper. It's the one day when the brother-in-law bends down to put on the shoes, helps with the suit, assists in mounting the horse, etc. The younger brother-in-law, sala, keeps heaping abuses on the older brother-in-law while getting his services. The jija in turn heaps abuses on the sala. Everyone laughs. No one minds the abuses. Not on such an occasion, not with this relationship.

Rinku was not voicing abuses, nor was our brother-in-law. They were educated people.

'Brother, when will bhabhi get here?' Rinku asked me.

'I don't know. You ask her.' I gave Rinku the mobile.

'She's just outside. She just entered the lane,' he told me, returning the phone.

He was ready in full attire. The drums were beating. The excitement increased. Jijaji had finished tying the pin scarf around his neck, and was holding the bridegroom's crown.

Just then Ayesha came down the stairs. Everyone's gaze rested on her. She was dressed in sky blue. She was the newest version of Ayesha for me so far. The gold of her jewellery served to heighten the natural fairness of her complexion.

'How do I look, Masterji?' she asked me softly. 'I chose your favourite colour.'

She knew my taste.

'Just like Aishwarya Rai,' said Rinku before I could speak. In spite of her low tone, he had heard her. 'Ayeshaji, you are looking like an angel.'

I did not say anything. My old weakness…of not speaking up in time.

Everyone's eyes would come and rest on her. She was the most attractive woman in the whole force of guests present. They could not help talking about her. The male guests from outside found some excuse to come inside and feast their eyes on her. A seven-year-old was throwing a tantrum that he would marry only Ayesha didi. Such was her magic.

Were they ill-intentioned people, these senior men who found an excuse to come into the house, coughing, to ogle her…or was this just a completely natural pull towards beauty?

Just then Sangita entered the house. The smell of her perfume and the sound of her anklets broke, as it were, the spell cast by Ayesha. Was this Sangita? I could not recognise her for a moment. Sangita was at her best in a shimmering peacock blue sari.

The centre of attraction was split into two now.

'Oh, my darling, may you be safe from the evil eye.' Bua circled Sangita's head with her hands and touched her own head.

'Oh didi, you took so long,' said Ayesha, taking her hand. Both of them looked at each other with a jealous admiration.

'I've been waiting here with my dry eyes for didi to come and put kajal in my eyes,' said Rinku.

'What a liar. The kajal was not even here and he claims to have been waiting for didi,' Meena came close to Sangita.

'There are liars upon liars here,' Sangita fired, looking at me. Amma, Rinku, Meena and I understood the barb even if other guests had no clue.

'You are looking lovely,' I said to Sangita as she passed me.

'That's what you must have said to Ayesha in private.' I could feel Sangita's temper.

'Ask her,' I replied.

Meena and Sangita put kajal in Rinku's eyes. The Maruti van and bus had computer-typed posters saying 'Rahul with Suman' stuck on them. Men, women and boys had started dancing to the drumbeats.

Just as the barat was ready to leave, Jayant, Sushil, Aslam and Firoz appeared. There were many policemen with them—the constables in uniform, others in plainclothes.

'Let's go straight to the bride's place, my lords!' I cried out in pleasure.

We embraced each other. I hugged Jayant and Firoz especially warmly, and they did the same. The hierarchy among us friends arose without my doing it. Sangita and Ayesha came and stood behind me.

'Where is bhabhi?' asked Jayant. He had not been present at my wedding and did not recognise Sangita.

'Sangita, this is Jayant.' I turned and introduced him. 'This is Sangita.'

'Bhabhiji, Jai Bhim,' Jayant greeted her according to custom.

'Jai Bhim,' Sangita replied.

'And she is her sister?' Jayant accounted for Ayesha.

Jayant had never any qualms in talking to strangers. He was equally comfortable with both men and women. He had no feelings of either attraction or revulsion towards women. He was free of male hang-ups from the beginning, not worrying whether women were impressed by him or not.

'No…' Ayesha came on the side of Sangita.

'You're here…' Sushil advanced towards Ayesha. He had a police officer's arrogance.

'This is my friend, Ayesha. You know her, Sushil.' Ayesha did not come forward, staying somewhat in the shelter of Sangita.

'This is Jayant, Aslam and Firoz, and this is Sushil, with the policeman's style,' I introduced each of them.

'I'm just coming didi.' Ayesha went towards her room. Sushil made to follow her but I stopped him.

'She is a prostitute, the bitch. I know her. She is our officer's mistress.' We were standing a little separate from others. This was Sushil's reply to my question if he knew her.

'Here, she is simply my guest. I am responsible for her. You will not know her.' My tone was hard.

'Is she a Muslim?' asked Aslam.

'Oh no, a Hindu bitch. A Bengali. Difficult to reach. High profile.' Sushil laughed. 'How did a person like you snare her? She's magic, the bitch—but obviously you can work still greater magic...'

'What fun—the wife and the mistress both side-by-side. The guy has luck.' Sushil teased.

'Sushil, you have no idea of my suffering.' I looked at him with sad eyes.

'Buddy, give me your suffering; I will bear it. It's a beautiful burden to bear.'

They were not in the mood to listen to anything serious.

'Have you planned the beer and so on?' Firoz tried to change the subject. He knew that soon Sushil and Aslam would descend to obscenities.

'Masterji, may I join you?' Ayesha appeared near us.

'Sure, sure, come,' I said in a dead voice. I did not want her there.

'Hi everybody.' This time she shook everyone's hand without hesitation. 'What did you say his name was?' This was not the timid Ayesha of a few minutes ago.

'Sushil.' Sushil said, coming forward. His face was greedy.

'You know Additional Police Commissioner B.N. Kaushik?' she asked fearlessly.

'Yes, of course. He is my immediate senior.' Sushil's voice now had a possessive pride.

'I am his mistress. An older man can do anything for a young woman…You get my drift, Sushil ji?' She paused, perhaps to see the effect her words were having.

'What do you mean?' Sushil seemed nonplussed.

'I mean that you are here as Masterji's friend and our guest. I would prefer if you forget about me for the rest of the function.' She went away without waiting for Sushil's reply. She had spoken so cordially that it took us some time to understand that it was a threat she had delivered.

'She is good at heart, just victimised by circumstances,' I said.

'Every prostitute has a story to tell,' said Aslam.

'She is very beautiful, very innocent,' Firoz said after a long time. 'You should stay away from her. As long as you control a fire, it is your friend. Once it is out of control, it can reduce you to ashes.' I understood Firoz's meaning. He was my sincere well-wisher.

'I prefer playing with fire.' This was Aslam. 'Love is not easy…it is a river of fire…it can only be crossed by drowning. Give me this fire, boss,' he said in a theatrical voice.

'You've started spouting poetry without drinking,' laughed Firoz.

'This sisterfucker won't give us drinks. The poetry won't wait around forever, will it?' Aslam said with feigned anger.

'Aslam, come with me.' We got two bottles of whiskey and four of beer from upstairs. We gave one bottle to the four plainclothesmen who had come with Sushil. One was enough for us. Only Aslam, Sushil and I were the drinkers. Jayant had left even beer. Firoz was unable to drink more than a peg of beer. We put more bottles in their car so that if the uniformed policemen wished to drink, they could do it away from us.

'Let's hurry. The barat must have reached,' said Jayant. We had had two pegs each already.

The barat had left by bus; many people had gone in their own cars. 'There's so much traffic in the city, it will take them an hour at least,' Firoz said in a groggy voice.

'Let's put a few more bottles in the car in case someone else comes.' I was already drunk, which was natural if you down drinks so fast.

'Yes, moderation should not mean stinginess,' said Firoz. He had become a Pathan with half a beer already.

'To exhibit poverty is worse than being poor,' Aslam added.

'I drank always on credit, thinking that one day my indebtedness will itself be a celebration.'

'I'll get some more. Jayant, come with me,' I cuffed Jayant on his shoulder.

'A poet should not get caught between fucking ignoramuses. I just have to do pointless free work,' Jayant said, coming with me.

'You are only doing the same as your fucking forefathers,' Sushil teased.

'At least they didn't clean fucking gutters,' Jayant replied, turning.

'The worst are the fucking butchers,' Firoz called out from the back.

'What happened with Nigar?' Jayant asked me as we left the others behind.

'What else? She got married and left for Hyderabad. He is still acting the fucking abandoned lover.' I was getting more drunk.

'Why did she leave?'

'The same caste business…This Firoz is a fucking coward. She had even said they could get married secretly with a Qazi but he did not agree. He said there would be meaningless violence and bloodshed. You want both to fucking love and then run away.'

'You are electrified,' he said

'Yes, bro. I'm drinking after a long time.' I tried to become steady.

'Drink less. Don't try to compete with Aslam and Sushil. Just now, when Firoz went to the bathroom, Aslam drank a bit of his beer and put whiskey in it.' He patted my shoulder. 'Look after yourself. It's your family function.'

'Oh, that's why he was staggering about so much…this should be fun. You take care of all of us today, you police officer. Why, isn't this your family as well, isn't Rinku your brother as well?'

'Fine, fine. Make me labour away. It might have been easier for me to have taken a few drinks too.' Jayant was laughing.

'Then go ahead, have a drink. Who has stopped you? It's your brother's wedding.' My mouth was getting carried away with me.

'Once you start, you can find an occasion everyday…It's difficult to stop, but easier to not start.'

'She is really very beautiful,' Firoz was saying when we returned with the bottle. They were still talking about Ayesha.

'There's no doubt about it. I have never seen a more attractive prostitute.' Jayant agreed with Firoz. 'Nigar fails before her,' he provoked Firoz.

'That…that fraud, what does she have to give in front of this one…this one is the Kohinoor…that one was glass. Not even glass, stone.' Firoz had fallen for Jayant's bait.

'You haven't seen her naked, or you would faint.' I wanted to stop myself but I could not. That's why I did not like alcohol. It had awakened my male bragging, whereas women still hide their bragging even among themselves.

'He has enjoyed himself, obviously,' Aslam shouted. 'Pretending to be a saint all this time.'

'Believe me, friends. I only looked at her, I didn't do…' my voice was full of shame. It was pointless to try to explain.

'We are suckling children, aren't we?' Firoz hit me on the shoulder.

'Well, believe me or not, friends, but that's the truth.' I was trying to get back in control.

'No one is a bigger motherfucking idiot than you, if it is true,' Aslam said with a gesture of rejection.

'When the senses get aroused, reason takes a backseat,' Jayant added. 'How was yours wide awake?'

'It's getting late, pal. Let's go now.' I tried to change the subject.

'Stop, bro.' Sushil stopped me. 'Rinku will get what he's going to get. We're here because of you.'

'Sushil, we'll have some fun in the barat, buddy.'

Sushil had been drinking away steadily. He had not taken part in the conversation. Since the moment Ayesha had threatened him, he had been a bit lost. Had he become scared?

'Bro, I have a nagging question…a fucking woman… when is she at her most beautiful?' Sushil pressed my hand as if to tell me something. 'Answer this question, then we'll go.'

'You're drunk.' I tried to save myself, if he was asking about Ayesha.

'No, I'll move only after you answer. Here is my promise.' Sushil literally planted a foot on the ground. I had to laugh at his childishness.

'Now you're going to have to tell him, or he won't remove his foot.' Aslam and Firoz both added fuel to the fire.

'No, I am not like that.' Some thought made Sushil move his foot.

I felt strange. How unpredictable people could be!

'Well, according to me…' I began and looked into their eyes. Everyone's eyes had curiosity, eagerness, restlessness. Even Jayant's. 'Just a moment after she has released her nectar, with someone she loves and gives full consent to.'

'Excellent, excellent!' Jayant patted me on the back. 'Our friend is reading Vatsyayana?'

'And at her ugliest?' Sushil asked, silencing him.

'No one is ugly, not woman, not man…Yes, they can be violent.'

'When?'

'Just a second or two before releasing her nectar.' I was in full form, either because of the pleasure of speech-making, or my male arrogance.

I had not read the *Kamasutra* but I had observed the experience of women many times over. Based on these observations, right or wrong as might be, I had experienced the leg-thrashing violence of women just before they came and the incomparable innocent, sweet beauty just after.

'Ayesha is also violent?' Firoz asked.

'Ayesha is a decent girl,' I said carefully. She was my friend.

'There's a diamond in every stone. There's a worm in every innocent smile,' said Sushil.

'Muktibodh was a Brahmin,' I said.

'All Brahmins are not bad,' Sushil agreed.

'Not only did he marry a non-Brahmin, he de-casted himself,' Jayant added.

'Is Ayesha a Brahmin too?' Sushil asked.

Everyone's eyes echoed the question. I kept quiet.

CHAPTER TEN

Weber Arrives

Then we got in the police car and reached the place the barat was supposed to collect. We danced to our heart's fill that night. Ayesha too. Sangita did not dance, but she seemed happy.

'I won't be able to live without you, Sangita.' I pulled her away by the hand to one side. 'Don't punish me for the mistakes I did not make. My life has no stable happiness—my misfortune.' I am not sure how I had the courage to say all this.

She listened quietly to me standing before her with folded hands.

'It would have been better if you had said this without being drunk,' she said, and went back into the crowd of people.

I could not blame Sangita; she was completely right. But where was I wrong? What could I do? Why was I unable to explain to Sangita?'

The wedding was wrapped up successfully. The pandit had recited the Gayatri mantra instead of the wedding 'seven steps' during the fire ceremony. The Buddhist monk had done his bit. Unlike the pandit, he did not need to wait for the auspicious moment. With the help of the Panchsheel and the Trisharan, Rahul and Suman were tied together in a social union.

Is this indissoluble union called marriage any more than that, a social institution? I gave it the name of 'tying up' based on a 'common minimum programme'. I did not consider it indissoluble either. Instead of a faith in its permanence, what I had was an honest striving to make it permanent.

The barat came back around noon. The women had returned at night itself. There was a riot, so to speak, at home all over again. Mother did a door-entry ritual for Rinku and Suman. Then Meena and Bari bua took Suman to a different room. Rinku went to their new room and fell asleep. The two of them had been up all night.

I went to my room upstairs. Ayesha was in the next room. Is she still sleeping? I wondered and knocked on her door. No one answered. I pushed the door gently and it opened. Ayesha was sitting on the floor in a reflective pose. She was mumbling something, or was praying for something.

The whole day passed with me doing nothing. The men were busy playing cards, and the women in cooking and gossip. One of the main topics of conversation for them was the dowry. As soon as it was evening, the men opened their bottles. Playing cards the whole day was a way of waiting for the evening.

The youngest mami's voice had not been heard the whole day. Then I heard it finally broaching the subject of dowry.

'Oh didi, are the bride's family misers? They've given no dowry at all?' She had observed a Matador van that accompanied Rinku and Suman, which seemed to have only the bride's clothes.

'Is that right, no dowry?' said the middle mami. 'They've covered the girl in gold.'

'How much gold is there altogether?' asked the oldest mami.

'Fifty *tolas*...'

'Jewellery of one and a half to two lakhs,' said the older bua.

'So, will she set up her home with jewellery? There have to be other things surely,' said the oldest mami, making a face.

'Brother does not like the practice of dowry. He told them no at the very beginning.' The oldest bua said this without enthusiasm. She was taking her brother's side without wishing to. Everyone expected her to change anytime now.

'Brother-in-law is a decent man,' said the oldest mami. 'Everyone claims to oppose dowry, but the bride's family should have their own pride.'

'They probably did not themselves want to give anything. They found the excuse in brother-in-law. The poorest have the most defiance.' This was the youngest mami's attack. 'Would someone have stopped them if they really tried to give?'

'You are right there,' agreed older bua quietly.

'Ladies!' Father called out loudly on entering the house. After waiting a few seconds, he proceeded inside. In that time, those who veiled themselves before him pulled their saris down on their faces and turned away. 'Are you plotting to blow up the nation?' Father looked at the oldest mami.

'Now you are all-in-all. No one listens to our sister-in-law,' the youngest mami attacked him with a laugh.

'What are you saying, dear? Think a little before you speak.' This was her husband, the youngest mama. He held two suitcases.

'Come, children, play outside…Lata dear, take them all outside.' Lata herded them all out.

'Amma, this is 5,00,000 cash, given by the bride's family,' the youngest mama said, going up to Amma. His voice had the pride of family, and then *biradari* in it. 'Besides this, there is furniture and a car…' he said, giving the keys. Meanwhile, Papa was sitting silently on a cot.

We did not hear the youngest mami's voice the whole day after this. She was seen once saying something to the youngest mama. She seemed to be asking to go home and he was saying no.

My friend from Germany, P.C. Weber, also arrived in the evening. He was a university lecturer, and had come to India on a research project. His topic was India's caste system.

He wanted to meet some Dalit authors. He was going to go to Maharashtra, Tamil Nadu and Karnataka after our city. I had emailed him about Rinku's wedding. He had shown great interest in observing the wedding. However, because of technical snags with his flight, he reached a full thirty-six hours late.

Vedprakash also came in the evening. He had been unable to come before because of his mother's illness.

'It's been ages since we met...let Rinku's wedding be the excuse,' he said, putting his arms around my neck.

'Let me call Jayant...But he has left drinking.'

'It's not necessary to drink, we can just meet.' He had spread himself out on the bed. 'Call Sushil, too, he won't say no to you. If Firoz and Aslam can also come, the group will be complete.'

I called everyone on their mobiles. Surprisingly, they all showed up. Arrangements had been made in the next room for Weber. When I took Vedprakash and reached there, we found Ayesha there. Weber knew excellent Hindi and Ayesha had no difficulty in making friends. She had described herself as a social worker and Weber was very interested. Weber was about forty years old, or maybe a little older. I always have trouble deciding on the age of White people. Ayesha was having no trouble whatsoever talking to him, explaining perhaps about the wedding and its rituals.

CHAPTER ELEVEN

We Friends

All of us were sitting together again. We were in the same room where, many years ago, Vandana had slapped me. The scene swam before my eyes for a moment. Those university days full of talk, full of the indefatigable energy to do something, full of nothing but sitting together quietly with each other…those days were all past. In the days since, many of us had gone here and there, many had come from here and there. Many events had transpired. Life had been running on soundlessly.

Are we all helpless to simply watch and experience what is passing? Are we ever able to do more than just observe? Is that our very tragedy?

Weber and two of my relatives had joined us; the relatives had come unasked. I wanted to exclude them but could not find a way to do so.

Ayesha went downstairs, and was not seen again all night. Maybe she went to sleep with Amma.

'Birpal Singh Jatav was killed. Someone shot him.'

Sushil had looked at Vedprakash with some hatred as he told us this. We had all been struck dumb hearing this.

'When?' asked someone in a low voice.

'Six months ago.' Sushil told us the details.

Birpal Singh had become quite notorious in police circles. He was called 'Encounter King'. The crime graph fell dramatically in whichever district he was posted. Criminals would simply leave the district. In one such encounter, someone fired at him. The scandal was that the firing was done not by a criminal, but by a police inspector. The bullet found in the postmortem was a government-issued bullet. The concerned policeman had even admitted to his crime before the search committee. He had told the search committee clearly that he could not clean the dirty dishes of a Chamar, or listen to abuses from a Chamar. All police officers oppress their juniors, but these officers were upper caste.

'Who was Birpal?' Weber had been listening quietly.

'He was our friend, a senior police officer.'

'Really shameful…that a responsible police officer be killed just because of caste.' Weber looked disturbed.

'This is a common occurrence in our villages and backward areas. Banwarilal has seen many such incidents,' one of my relatives put forward his own view.

He was a distant uncle, but felt comfortable with me because we were close in age. He was a patwari, or accountant, by profession and very talkative. He had squelch in his eyes and his hair was greasy with oil.

'Which Banwarilal?' Weber wanted to know.

'His own name is Banwarilal.' I had been anticipating the question. 'He has been using his name Banwarilal instead of "I" from the beginning.'

'It's all a fallacy…who is Banwarilal and who is Weber… these are all superficial distinctions,' the uncle spoke again.

'Really interesting…you are an interesting person,' Weber chuckled.

The depression produced by Birpal's news was scattered with laughter.

'And any news of K. Rajesh?' asked Firoz, downing his beer.

'Oh, he was a Mallah. No one knew about him.' Sushil gave a hoot of laughter. 'He was also a weird one. His bad days began when he addressed the Mallahs to rise up on the occasion of Phoolan Devi's martyrdom day. The newspapers made a big deal of it. If he had been a non-Dalit, this would all have gone in his favour…he would have been called a progressive policeman. Instead, his decline started. Gautam turned out to be clever in this regard.'

'You are up to date on everyone,' Jayant laughed. He was drinking juice. I had got an imported mixed fruit juice keeping him in mind. 'What happened with Gautam? Where are you off to?' he asked watching me get up.

'Just a minute.' I got a second bottle. 'There was a little left in yesterday's bottle, so we finished that. Now we will open a new one.'

'Don't worry. Today there will be nothing left. Banwarilal drinks a lot.'

Uncle made Weber laugh again.

Weber's laugh set Sushil laughing. Seeing them both, I gave a loud guffaw. Then everyone was laughing, save uncle; he was used to others laughing in his company.

'What happened with Gautam?' This time the question was from Weber.

'Nothing much; he is a very practical and flexible person. He had become the special man of the biggest funder of the party of Dalits and Backward Classes. He had to pay for it by getting married a second time. He did not divorce his first wife but got her consent; she was a simple housewife.'

'But this is illegal…is it not?' Weber looked at Sushil.

'There is so much that is illegal. Add one more thing. When the husband and wife agree, who will act the priest to interfere?' Sushil replied.

'He should have got a divorce,' said Firoz.

'It's not as easy for Hindus,' said Sushil. 'They would be half-dead running around the courts. Then, the first wife did not want to leave him either.'

'He could get caught for this one day,' said Firoz, tossing his head as if he was done with the subject.

'Nothing will happen to him. High caste people are everywhere,' Sushil's eyes had something like contempt, arising perhaps from envy, as he said this. 'It's we who meet obstacles at every turn.'

'Now wait a minute, Sushil, don't get started, please. Look, buddy, there are guests here,' I interrupted. 'None of this in front of Mr Weber.'

Some flies had entered even at this late hour and were buzzing around.

'But Sushil is correct. He is a sensible and smart officer. If he wants to say something on the subject of reservations, that is his personal right.'

Vedprakash taking his side made Sushil very pleased, which he could not hide. Vedprakash gave him a nice opportunity by expanding the context of the whole subject.

Sushil addressed Weber directly. 'Mr Weber, you don't know that we have hierarchy and caste difference within untouchables.'

'Sushil, my dear friend…Mr Weber, he is not incorrect. Everyone looks down on his caste. Caste Hindus do so, of course, but when Dalits themselves do so, how can they blame the caste Hindus for discrimination—what do you say, Mr

Weber?' Vedprakash poured oil on the flame, as it were, by adding to Sushil's point.

'It's all very strange.' Mr Weber's attitude had become like the United Nations.

'I am a Bhangi, Mr Weber. You know Bhangi means sweeper. Chamar and Khatik, both untouchables, treat us as more untouchable than themselves,' Sushil's anger had grown with his drinks.

'Now look, Sushilji, don't call Khatiks untouchable.' Uncle was also drunk. 'Banwarilal is not an untouchable. His caste is not untouchable.'

'No one is an untouchable! Stop all this nonsense.' I got annoyed. Have you come here to meet or to fight?'

'You cannot stop Banwarilal. Even God cannot stop Banwarilal. He will tell you that Chamars have gobbled up all the reserved places. Banwarilal will speak up,' uncle pounded his fist on his palm as if a judge was controlling his courtroom.

'Uncle, will you keep quiet…You say you are not an untouchable, so why are you concerned with reservations?'

'Well, son. So Banwarilal has lost his caste and also lost his reserved seats.' Sushil had been bad enough. Now this uncle had stepped into the field. 'This is a joke. They will include us in the untouchables but will not give us reservations.'

'His arguments are not wrong, Mr Weber. The scheduled castes include many castes. Reservations should apply to all of them.' Vedprakash began to interfere again. 'No one caste should monopolise them. If they do, then who is to fault upper castes?'

'Yes, now S.C. means not scheduled caste, but Sirf (only) Chamar. S for "Sirf", C for Chamar,' Sushil spoke rudely.

'And you want to make it Sirf Chuhda. S for Sirf and C for Chuhda.' Jayant, quiet all this time, made a counterattack. He stopped Sushil's unfettered steed before I could. And he did so calmly, without the last excitement. He kept sipping his juice calmly, though I could see the tension on his temples.

'Mr Weber, it should be clear enough but we cannot see it clearly because of our self-interests,' I signalled Weber to turn his attention to me. 'In North India, the Chamar population is so large that, naturally, we see Chamars everywhere.'

'You cannot speak up candidly like us,' Sushil said sarcastically. 'You are always being tactful either with Brahmins, or to Chamars.' His attack on me was because of Vandana and Sangita, no doubt.

Weber had had the most to drink but was the most sober. Aslam and Firoz were listening quietly, as if the matter did not concern them at all. Aslam was quiet, in spite of his heavy drinking only because of the gravity of the discussion—otherwise he would have been spouting Urdu poetry long ago. We had already finished one bottle.

'Just as the Mala and Madiga have divided up reserved seats between them in Andhra Pradesh, so could we in North India.' This was a new voice in the noise, my relative's, a distant brother. He had come from Haryana and taught law in a college. 'The Bhangis and Khatiks are locked in battle in Haryana. So much so that they have no political existence. No party is sensitive to their needs. Only caste rules everywhere, or else the Jatavs.'

'Fine, then, let's have a census according to caste and give everyone their share according to their numbers.' Jayant was still cool. But his point stunned everyone. 'I say, give reservations to the Brahmins as well, and to Thakurs also. Count everyone according to caste and give everyone their portion.' Jayant looked at Vedprakash.

'Bhaiya, should I get more meat,' Lata came to the door and called me.

'No, sister, no. There's plenty here,' said the Haryana cousin.

'Lata, my daughter, bring more, this will not be enough… Banwarilal will eat meat with force!'

Lata went laughing downstairs.

'There can be no end to this debate.' Vedprakash downed the remaining drink in his glass in one gulp and put the glass upside down on the table.

'That is why I did not want it to start. It only increases bitterness and destroys cordiality,' I agreed with Vedprakash.

'We should keep quiet to increase goodwill among people…that's what upper castes tell us and caste Dalits repeat. That's what your advice is,' Sushil sounded depressed.

'As soon as someone asks for their rights, of course, there will be bitterness. No one gives away their share willingly.' This was uncle again.

'You keep quiet, uncle. You think you belong to the scheduled castes.' I tried to undermine his confidence. 'You've taken the discipleship of some Hindu leader, I've heard.'

'So what? So what if Banwarilal believes it or not... there are others. There's you.' He was waving his hands in the air.

'So, who had forbidden the other castes to not study, not compete in government exams. Whoever studied, made it.' I waved my hands too. 'Even among the Jatavs, those who did not study, still live in their illiteracy.'

'Isn't this to blame the victim, to accuse those who are already downtrodden?' Sushil said. 'It's the state's job to give everyone an education and an equal chance.'

'So, quarrel with the state. What did the Chamars steal from you? Whatever they've got is through their hard work and struggle, and their awareness,' Jayant proposed in a quiet tone again.

I was jealous of his calmness, that he was able to remain unruffled even on this provocative occasion.

Sushil was not wrong, neither was Jayant. Uncle's points were not baseless either. Sushil had been spurned by many officers who were Chamars when he wanted to feel an insider with them. Because of this, he looked at all Chamars as one. He had told me often that when officers who were Chamars had parties, they did not call him. I had tried to make him understand that, in fact, when people belong to the same sub-caste, they often turn out to be related and then become a closed group. Plus, it's anyone's right to call whoever they like to their parties.

Every point of Jayant's was logical. He had told me that Sushil's posting in the city had been arranged by a minister of the Chamar caste; Sushil himself had told me that. Then, at every party he would abuse the Chamars in the same way he had done just now, and this had stopped the invitations to him everywhere. Jayant had said that if Sushil actually wanted to do something for the Bhangis, he should do the work and stop talking. The Chamars were busy, constantly doing work among themselves.

But was that the same reason that upper caste Hindus did not want to call Dalits to their parties? Did the Dalits behave like Sushil?

'Mr Weber, the Brahmins and the Chamars are the same for us. Neither will the Brahmins help us, nor will the Chamars,' Sushil showed his last card. 'This country will never be free of casteism. The Brahmin will help the Brahmin, and the Chamar will help the Chamar.'

'And the Bhangi will help the Bhangi,' Jayant added again.

'Hey brothers, you have spoilt the drinking, we Muslims are so much better...Why have you taken up this topic, can't we talk of this Ayesha instead?' Aslam's was an invitation to end an unwelcome topic and start a fresh one. 'What marvellous eyes, wherever they look, they produce sighs. Where is the blue-eyed beauty today?'

'Don't bring up that fucking prostitute, Aslam,' Sushil threatened Aslam.

'Sushil...mind your language.' I ground my teeth. 'Don't forget that she is my friend and a guest in this house.'

Sushil was quiet after a 'Sorry'. Aslam did not mention her again. I read the questions in Weber's eyes. They were directed at me. But he didn't ask me, and I said nothing further about her.

'You must have enjoyed yourselves yesterday?' Vedprakash broke the silence.

Though summer was coming, there was a chill in the air. The chill had increased after I spoke angrily. No one answered Vedprakash. Maybe it was a useless question and no one could think of anything to say, or they were waiting for each other to speak.

'Aslam, what have you thought about yourself…how long will you do this agent's work?' Firoz went on a new turn in the conversation.

'I'm better than you, Master. I've bought my own house and car. I don't live in a rented house like you or get knocked around on a government bus.' The conversation thread broke down.

'I want to open a small charitable school,' Sushil interrupted to say. 'But I can't do it openly.'

'It's a good plan,' Jayant said in support. 'Better than a school, a small hospital perhaps.'

'No, a school…then there can be branches of the school,' I agreed with Sushil.

'But it will need a lot of time and hard work,' said Jayant.

'And none of us have the time.'

'Then?' Sushil looked at Jayant.

'I feel that the beginning should be made with a small dispensary, in a poor neighbourhood,' Firoz advised. 'There are so many such neighbourhoods in the city and small villages too.'

'You can ask the doctors you know for help, just to start with,' Aslam said to me.

'Sangita could also help,' Jayant said.

'I can't say anything about her. She is divorcing me.'

'What!' the exclamation was universal.

'But why?' Sushil was on his feet, shaking my shoulders. Sushil was an especially emotional being. He could give his life to a friend, and take an enemy's life as well.

'My family did not tell her about my marriage to Vandana.'

'Yes, but why did you not tell her?' Firoz asked.

'I tried to tell her, but did not succeed because of a misunderstanding.' I told them the whole story of that evening.

'I will talk…to Bhabhi,' Sushil said. 'She won't find a better man than you.'

'We'll talk to her too,' everyone said.

Then the conversation went back to the school to be set up, and from there reached the dispensary. The talk now centred on the name of the dispensary, its location, and how to set it up. Sushil was making a new beginning. We were happy to be his supporters. It is the time for teams, not individuals.

'Bodhisatva Sunit Hospital,' Jayant suggested the name. Sushil opposed it, saying that Jayant brought in caste everywhere, but Jayant proved correct. It was a mark of the first step taken in public service.

This was our simple achievement during Rinku and Suman's wedding. A reception was held the next day. Sangita came with Sudesh chacha and his wife Sukhjot. Kalra, Rana and other friends, who could not come on the wedding day, also came.

'This bitch is here too,' Rana said to me, seeing Ayesha standing with Rinku and Suman.

Ayesha had seen them too, and had chosen to go and stand in a safe place with the bride and groom. When Kalra and Rana went to the stage to shake hands with Rinku and give their presents, Kalra pulled Ayesha's hands and forced her to come beside him. Rana sniggered upon seeing this. I couldn't stand it.

'Please, Kalra sir,' Ayesha gestured to him to get down from the stage. 'Others are waiting.' She spoke with exaggerated courtesy. Kalra and Rana quietly got down and mingled with the crowd.

'Who was that rude man?' Sangita came to me after some time. I had not expected that she would see it all. But I was pleased that Sangita had voluntarily come up to me.

'That man.' I turned towards Kalra theatrically. 'He is Ayesha's boss, I think.' I tried to look innocent.

'You think…Meaning you don't know?' Sangita's brows were furrowed.

'No, I'm meeting him for the first time.' I was worried at what Sangita might think of me, seeing Kalra's crude behaviour. I thought it best to appear ignorant about him. She might ask Ayesha directly about him, then it would be my 'I think' that could save me.

'You are a liar by nature,' Sangita said, stamping her foot. 'You were talking to him for ages until 10 minutes ago.'

Trying to save myself had not worked. It might have been better to have told her the whole truth to begin with. I had to hide my one lie under a hundred more—wasn't this the trouble with lies anyway?

I was tempted to rid my burden by telling Sangita everything. But once she knew about Ayesha being a prostitute, would she behave normally with me? I actually did not want to accept that role of Ayesha's, or present her to others as that. Deep in my consciousness was also the thought that Ayesha in an innocent friend's role could be of more help to me than Ayesha in her old role. Ayesha's beauty and straightforward behaviour were helping me in coming close to Sangita. Sangita was getting upset with me but also attracted. She did not want to see me become someone else's.

How could Amma's prophecy fail? I was unutterably happy in the hope that my lack of pretense was making a way to her. Sangita had watched me for an hour—was this inconsiderable? At the same time, there was something still proving to be an obstacle. What was it? My lying? That was simply because of my insecurity, set in motion by Ayesha's presence.

Sangita went back to Sudesh uncle and stood with them. I could say nothing; there was nothing to be said.

The reception had a DJ floor on one side. Children, old doddering people, youth, women and girls—all were dancing. Punjabi songs resounded loudly. Popular songs were blaring at full volume. Great singers such as Sukhbir, Mika, JGB,

Harbhajan Man and Hansraj Hans were being played as loudly as possible.

Weber, Aslam, Jayant, Sushil, Kalra, Rana—all were dancing. Firoz was cursing Nigar loudly; someone had made him intoxicated today.

Punjabi culture had taken over the city, from its music to its food. The city was different than 20 years ago. Though it was the capital, it was populated with villages. It was like a banyan tree that permitted many trees to flourish under it. This had changed in the last 20 years, in both the city's body and soul. Instead of *saag* and *puri* you had *chhola*, *matar-paneer* and *naan*. The sitting in rows to be served had been transformed into the buffet. The aromatic cups made of clay and the wet leaf-platters had been replaced by china plates washed and re-washed in dirty water. The relatives who ran up and down the rows, urging you to have one more *puri*, more *laddu*, *barfi*, *imarti* even when you stopped them forcibly, had vanished. These same relatives had now become guests. Waiters in white shirts and black trousers walked around refilling serving bowls and removing tubs of dirty plates. Guests did not trust that there would be a chance for a second helping, and heaped their plates the first time around.

The market place had redefined not only our relationships, but our needs as well. We were helpless and could just observe and experience.

The old proverb that necessity is the mother of invention could be discarded. The new proverb that could hold sway was that invention was the mother of necessity. This new discourse told us that girls were unlikeable because of the smell of perspiration, and young women had begun to believe it. Now they had to go further. The discourse was telling the young women that instead of other shampoos, if you use this shampoo your hair will be silkier and straighter. And most of all, grease-free, grease being what young men hate the most. Young women were, therefore, using the given shampoo to keep young men attracted to them. A grandmother whose son did lime whitewashing did not want her granddaughter to marry unless the groom's family dealt only in foreign wall paint. To have a cold drink meant to have Coca-Cola. In this new discourse, there was first an invention, then the development of everyone's needs to consume that invention. The new proverb had turned invention and needs around.

Was it totally bad, though? Our lives were certainly more comfortable. Now we did not have to book a television or a car, and wait years in advance. Young women were freed from days of discomfort and shame, locked up in their homes during their periods. Young men did not need to go searching for milk and almonds. They could get a high-protein food supplement that would develop their muscles beautifully.

The Punjabi songs had a rhythm that produced an excitement in the body. It was a folk music form that had made space for itself in the world. The folk music form was built solely on an anti-Brahmin culture. Otherwise, priests had so far excluded music, dance and theatre from 'culture', considering them to be part of the culture of Sudras.

Wherever the rule of Brahmins had weakened, various forms of folk music and dance had blossomed forth.

As the night progressed, guests left one by one. The marquee was still bathed in glaring white lights, but its attractiveness was gone now that it was deserted. It had been beautiful only because of the people in it.

'We will sit one day in May for planning the hospital.' We friends decided as we said our goodbyes. I had asked for a month because I was tied up with Weber, and then a project. Then Baba Saheb Ambedkar's birthday on 14th April meant many programmes.

April was a blessed month for us as Jesus' birth was for Christians.

I returned to my university flat after two or three days. In that lonely, sad place I had a private corner that gave me happiness. Amma had stayed back. She had wanted to come but Father had not let her.

CHAPTER TWELVE

Firoz

Life came back to its old routines: the same classes, the same long pathways.

'Will you find some stability or keep going around like a lost lover calling out to their beloved?' I asked Firoz.

He had come over on Saturday to stay with me. He often spent the weekend with me and left for college from there on Monday morning.

'I doubt whether I can find anything,' said Firoz in a depressed voice. 'She has abandoned me…I had gotten used to her. I measure every girl by her standards. I am going to ruin, I know it.' His face had become long and drawn.

In spite of a dark complexion and ordinary features, Firoz was unusually attractive, perhaps because of his deep voice or his open, honest behaviour.

'You need stability to survive.'

I was amazed that I, whose suffering was caused by a lack of 'stability', was advising Firoz to find that very thing. Was this but our natural hypocrisy?

'So who the hell is surviving?' Firoz's dead voice disturbed me. Had he become suicidal?

'We should not live in a half-dead way, Firoz,' I said, comforting him with my arm on his shoulder.

He was a lovely person and it was my heart's desire that he stay with me my whole life. Was this simply a selfish wish? It was the same wish I had for Sangita, and perhaps Ayesha.

'And you?' He searched my eyes.

'I do have a ray of hope...' I hesitated and spoke carefully. It was a delicate moment and the wrong words could have hurt Firoz. 'Sangita could possibly come back soon...she is going to have my baby.'

'Really?' He smiled, though his voice was still depressed. 'Who knows but Nigar might come back. I have a ray of hope too.' He beat his fingers on the table.

'Is this just a concoction of your imagination or do you have something to base it on?' I was curious to know if he had something new to share.

'She is not happy...I met her in Hyderabad University last month.' As he looked into my eyes, I understood that my guess was wrong. He was clutching at straws.

'Children?' I asked to push further, straightening my collar.

'She has two daughters.' He tried to smile. 'That's why she does not get along with her husband. He wants a son to look after his business. Son, my foot, the motherfucker wants a manager.'

'Did you ask her about taking a divorce?' I was so fed up with my own sentimentalism that I could not bear anyone else to be swayed by pure sentiments.

'She won't ask for one but she was saying that her husband will himself divorce her.' He had a lost look in his eyes as he saw a dream that was never going to come true.

I could not tell him that. He was not merely clutching at straws. He was seeing a mirage in the desert.

'But suppose her husband marries again without divorcing her?'

He was silent at my question.

'I did not think of that,' he said without feeling.

'I introduced you to Vaishali at Rinku's reception…you remember?' I knew he remembered. The special thing about Vaishali for him would have been that her face resembled Nigar quite a bit.

'You remember?' I repeated.

'Yes, yes, why not,' he sounded embarrassed.

'Will you marry her?' I could see from his countenance that he had thought of exactly the same thing.

'What are you saying, pal?' His eyes showed surprise and disbelief, and also expectation.

'Seriously. Her family will have no objection…they are quite modern.'

Vaishali's older sister Vishakha had married a Christian young man. Vaishali taught in a public school, and was convent-educated. Vaishali's father, Pahariya Sahab, was the first among Khatiks to convert to Buddhism.

'Still…' he murmured.

'Would you rather go back to Bihar to live, or is it something to do with caste?' I was irritated at his embarrassment. He wanted what I suggested but could not say so.

'I am hardly a Sayyid or Pathan to be casteist! I am an Ansari whose ancestors were also Chamars just three or four generations ago,' he said without hesitation. 'What caste or sect do the poor and helpless have?'

'Well then?'

'…'

'Come on, pal, say the word.' I was now truly irritated.

'Vaishali looks just like Nigar, she even sounds like Nigar.' He got embroiled in the past. 'You should ask Vaishali first.'

'Fine, but don't forget that she is Vaishali, not Nigar.' I thought it important to emphasise that.

Do we not always love our own imagined people, and not actual people? I was afraid that Firoz was saying 'yes' not to Vaishali but to his imagined Nigar. But was Nigar not imagined as well? Was Vandana not my imagination, which is why I could never be one with her? Sangita and Ayesha attracted me because they fulfilled my imagined roles for them. Can we, in fact, ever love other people for themselves or just love our own images of them?

I talked to Vaishali's father, and then to Vaishali about Firoz. 'It's up to Vaishali,' Pahariya Sahab said without objection. But Vaishali had said no. She was in love with another young man and wanted to marry him. I told Firoz everything.

'As you can see, I am not fated to have stability in my life. What can I do?' he laughed, his voice echoing as if in a ruined building.

I was worried for him.

But time reveals its secrets slowly. About six months later, Vaishali phoned me and wanted to meet Firoz.

'He was an upper caste Hindu idiot.' I had asked about the young man she was going to marry. When I asked if he was a Brahmin, she told me that he used 'Tyagi' as a surname. 'He was a medieval man.'

Firoz and Vaishali got married after six months of going out. It was a day of great happiness for us.

CHAPTER THIRTEEN

A Dream

I had arranged for Weber to stay in a guest house after Rinku's wedding. I wanted him to participate in the Ambedkar Jayanti celebrations in the city and meet people.

But Weber had his whole itinerary chalked out from before he even left Germany. He had to be in Nagpur on 14th April. He was an organized person, as all foreign intellectuals are. I realised that he would not stay, and that it was pointless to even ask him to.

I believe that one cannot burden others with one's own feelings and desires. One must be democratic in feelings and desires as well. But is this even possible in the Indian environment? Isn't it true that the punishment for being rational is to become a foreigner and outsider to one's own society and period? Albert Camus' protagonist in *The Stranger* has to suffer a death sentence because he is free of sloppy sentiments. Camus' stranger status was in 1942 France and, gradually with time, he achieved freedom from it. So how long were we Indians going to continue to be uncivilised and primitive?

'It's an extraordinary experience to witness the Ambedkar celebrations in Nagpur,' I told Weber.

'Have you ever gone there on the day?' Weber perhaps saw the brightness in my eyes.

'Certainly, many times. It's like a pilgrimage for us.'

'Maybe like Haj,' he smiled and stretched out on a chair.

'It might become like that for the whole nation, and the world, in the coming decade.' I pressed my folded knee.

'Amen…' Weber smiled. 'You are religious. I mean, I feel that religion for you is…it's just a thought. I may be wrong,' he hesitated.

'Religion is the need of the hour, Mr Weber.'

I wanted to say that while we could personally even be atheists, we could not be non-religious either in life or in death. Whether we like it or not, we all have a religion into which we are born, and in which we die. God might be irrelevant in our lives, but religion influenced our whole social life and often determined it. After this is understood, we are free to challenge religion and to reject it, but the first step is to acknowledge it. I did not want to argue about all this just then.

'Is religion a game of power?' Weber tried to look into my mind.

'No, it is a conflict of identity…and every conflict in the Buddhist world has a resolution (vimarsh).' I spoke calmly and without feeling, like Jayant. I had learnt this from Jayant—how to stay balanced even when passionately moved.

'Anyway, let it be.' Weber fathomed my reluctance to argue further. 'I have to meet many people in Nagpur…I'd like you to suggest some people I could meet.'

'Who is on your list?' I thought it best if he told me his plans first.

'Baburao Bagul, Namdev Dhasal, Lakshman Gaekwad and Arun Kumar Limale.'

'Very good, but you can't meet them all in Nagpur. They live in different parts of the state. You should also meet Loknath Yashwant, Pragya Lokhande, Urmila Pawar and Kishor Shantabai Kale.'

I gave him their addresses and phone numbers as he was leaving. Through a Dalit officer in the Ministry, I also made arrangements for his stay in a guest house in Nagpur.

Weber left for Nagpur on 10th April. Ayesha went with him. They had become good friends in this time.

'You are smart but, still, be careful,' I gave her a friend's advice at leaving. 'He is a foreigner; he may not know much about things here.' I was keen that nothing unpleasant transpire.

'People are the same everywhere, Masterji,' Ayesha replied to me gently. 'I am not afraid of men, but of women.'

I could sense her pain.

I got busy with my many responsibilities. Many associations and academies were organising programmes on this occasion. Dalit writers' unions were applying themselves to their familiar topics with new enthusiasm. A day could pass quickly in the making of posters, writing pamphlets and debating for hours.

If one's goal is clear then it's not just the day but a life that can pass quickly, before one realises it. Only in the absence of a goal does every moment of one's life transform itself into a hundred lives.

It was at the end of such a day. I had no idea when I ate or drank during the day of running around…maybe something at the wayside stall with my colleagues and students. I came back home and crashed.

'How long will we look towards the platforms and journals of upper castes…' Mohandas Naimishray is speaking as the main speaker of the People's Platform (Janvadi Vichar Manch). On the stage are Rajendra Yadav, Namvar Singh, Asghar Vajahat, Linda Hess and Laura Brueck…Hans Werner Wessler, Vishwanath Tripathi, Anamika, Maitreyi Pushpa, Jaiprakash Kardam, Chandrabhan Prasad, Tej Singh, Shyamlal Jaidiya, Kanwal Bharati, Rupnarayan Sonkar and Anita Bharati are also present. Rajendra Yadav is roaring with laughter; smoke from a pipe is flowing around his glasses…it has transformed his upper caste world into its own world…great. Namvar Singh is quietly picking up the edge of his dhoti and going to the back of the stage with mincing steps to spit out his tobacco, all while speaking. Vishwanath Tripathi is telling him to sit down.

'I am grateful that you all should have been so gracious as to be present at the book launch of an emerging author like me...' Roopnarayan Sonkar is saying humbly.

'It's the literature of Dalits, women and minorities that is the literature of tomorrow...' Rajendra Yadav is thundering.

'The bigger thing is not life's experience but consciousness,' Vishwanath Tripathi interrupts Rajendra Yadav to say.

'Economic emancipation is the only real emancipation,' Kanwal Bharati is roaring.

'We have to fight for economic freedoms alongside social ones...I could understand the reality of India thanks to Kabir,' Linda Hess is saying in clear Hindi in spite of her foreign accent.

Laura Brueck is smiling.

'God save women!' Anamika's voice has the rhythm of high breeding...

'The best cultural synonym for gender sensitisation is the dishonouring of men. We just need diversity in India, friends, nothing else...diversity is the Dalit Manifesto,' Chandrabhan Prasad in a black kurta and white churidar is waving his hands to explain...

Dr Dharmvir has arrived...Dr Dharmvir has arrived...

On the stage Rajendra Yadav is still puffing out smoke from his pipe; he pats the chair next to him, saying, 'Come, come, Dharmvir ji.'

'Oh, you are also here...' Namvar Singh minces up from the back and stands next to Dharmvir...

'Premchand had blue eyes...he was an adulterer...an adulterer...an adulterer...He bore children with Budhiya...I am only concerned with the story Kafan...But we have invited you here to speak on Kabir, not Premchand,' Jaiprakash is being abusive...

'We know well that Premchand was a scriptwriter (or clerk) for feudalism...he rode on a horse carriage, a paan in his mouth, to the office of Hans everyday...just as Rajendra Yadav, his pipe in his mouth, rides in his Tata Indica to the Hans office in Daryaganj every day. A driver called Kishan drives this horse carriage with a license plate of DLCCU 2072!'

'Well said, Dharmvir ji, well said! Dalit religious identity, pride, is all in your hands...'

A man in the audience, poor and lean, begins to dance on one leg...Anita Bharati explains that this is Bant Singh; the upper caste men in his village abused his daughter. When he opposed them, they cut off both his hands...he is waving his stumps in the air and dancing; he preaches Marxism. 'All around, society is dumb, in the village and the province...' he is singing, in a voice filled with agony…

'Please have a seat, Dharmvir ji…' Dr Dharmvir's arrival has sent excitement coursing through the audience; now he will start his recitation of love affairs. One spectator moves from one side of the hall to the opposite side; the audience is moving around…some are leaving one side of the hall to sit on the other…'Well-targeted, Dharmvir ji…excellent shot inside the house…' Brajpal Bharati of Bahujan Diversity Mission is calling out a 'hip, hip, hurray'. Prahladchand Das and Hiralal Rajasthani are requesting him to sit down quietly.

'Their stories are, of course, published in journals, but who reads them? We just turn the pages and move on, they keep abusing us,' a spectator is telling his neighbour, '…the great ajivak are against Kabir's loves. They are fighting to protect the honour of Dalit women…All are equal in Buddha's dhamma… the foundation of Dalit literature has to be Buddhist dhamma… Dr Dharmvir is the Sai Baba of the Dalits…' Dr Dharmvir keeps four fingers on his lips and watches…he is surprisingly silent, unlike himself. He says to Tulsiram, 'Tulsiram, why don't you teach Russian politics, why are you putting your foot into Dalit literature…'

H.L. Dusadh has stood up from the audience, 'We should give an opportunity to the youth…give them the sky to soar in!' Asgar Wajahat is congratulating Rupnarayan Sonkar on the publication of his autobiography…Laura Brueck and Wessler are also congratulating Sonkar, 'Well done, Mr Sonkar.' 'I am pleased,' says Rajendra Yadav and rises, 'that I have destroyed the upper caste ideology of Manu and made it democratic. I have seen my goals fulfilled in my lifetime…what could be a more meaningful happiness than that…' His voice is deep but trembling. On hearing him, an impressive personality raises his hand from the audience and stands up; he is wearing a three-piece suit…he looks as if he carries the whole world's glamour on his shoulders. The great man is walking with his polished shoes towards the stage; everyone on the stage stands up…they are surprised and hypnotised. The great man keeps advancing towards the stage. Rajendra Yadav has put his pipe on the table and, in spite of his problems, stands up with the help of his stick…Dr Dharmvir comes leaping…Chandrabhan Prasad is behind. The great man puts one hand on Chandrabhan Prasad's and the other on Dr Dharmvir Bharati's shoulders.

He moves on to Rajendra Yadav, 'You are my true partner, Rajendra, thank you…' the great man embraces Rajendra Yadav. 'Long live Baba Saheb Ambedkar…Long live the leader of the downtrodden, Dr Ambedkar…Long live the great Ambedkar!' Many children in the audience are shouting; they are running to come and touch the great man. Many children have entwined themselves at his feet. Some have found chocolates, toffees and books in the great man's pockets…

The great man is laughing, is chuckling…'I set out alone

for my goal but people kept joining me and the caravan grew…' Aslam is reciting poetry. 'No maddened love understood my speech, each one was a stranger in their own separate place… This social set up has no power to destroy us; we have made it, not that it has made us…' Aslam keeps reciting poetry…I am floating on top of Aslam…'big claws…a big curved beak like an eagle…caw caw…a voice like a crow's...a size bigger than a pigeon…what have I become…I am going on flying…The night is about to end…The dark is intense…caw caw caw…I perch on the railing of a house…the Valmiki neighbourhood… almost everyone is passed out in sleep…there is a light in 15 or so homes. It's Baba Saheb Ambedkar's anniversary, awake and arise…' A few people are banging on the door of every house… Advocate Bhagwandas in the front…No one is coming out… everyone continues to sleep…'Oh, let me sleep, I was possessed by the goddess all night,' a woman's voice calls out…'Go away, who is Ambedkar to us?' a harsh male voice calls out from somewhere…

'Long live the Bhangis, long live the Chamars…oppose anyone who stops them,' the people outside are shouting slogans…'We Bhangis have the same God…awake, awake… caw caw caw…' I fly off…the Jatav neighbourhood…The whole neighbourhood is blazing with light except for its largest, well-built houses…'Long live Baba Saheb Ambedkar…We have a new life, thanks to him…We were lower than animals,' the mother is combing the tresses of the daughter; the daughter has dreams in her eyes…'A truck is starting up outside…Our collections fell a little short or we would have had fifty instead of just twenty trucks to take everyone…' a male voice is telling another…'Delhi is far, after all…it's difficult to take everyone… I've heard there's a huge gathering at the Parliament House… are you going for the first time?'

'Yes, brother, I could never get time off from work before but this time I decided…Won't these people in the big houses get up…Don't they have to acknowledge Baba Saheb…oh well, they are the rich and beautiful…they think of themselves as bigger than Baba Saheb…Leave them… they are Hindus; they do the all-night worships at temples'… Caw caw caw…this is my nieghbourhood….there is a sign in front…'Khatiks' neighbourhood'…Dhanpat is getting ready to go vegetable shopping in the market…Caw caw caw…I go in front of Dhanpat…'Dhanpat, my cousin is aiming pebbles at me to chase me away…' He does not recognise me; he cannot understand my speech…I want to tell them all that today is Baba Saheb's anniversary…it's useless. 'Long live Sir Durbalnath, the Great', a procession is taking out a palki…a bird is lying in the palki, frail and injured…big claws…a big, curved beak…like an eagle…bigger than a pigeon…'Caw caw caw…' he replies in a soft and frail voice on hearing me…

That old bird is saying, 'Long live Baba Saheb…' The

crowd paused and then started shouting again, 'Long live Baba Saheb! Long live Durbalnath ji!' Some have started shouting, 'Victory to the Goddess, Victory to the Goddess, Victory to the Goddess…Victory to the whole body of followers…Victory to Shiva…Victory to Bhairon!' Liquor bottles have appeared… everyone is drinking…we have freedom…we are materialists… we are not anyone's slaves…all the neighbourhoods have united…the bottle falls from the hand and crashes near me…

I opened my eyes with a jerk. The birds were going wild on the Gulmohar tree outside. I looked lazily at the dawning light outside. I had not slept enough and my body was still stiff with exhaustion, but I made the effort and got up.

CHAPTER FOURTEEN

Aslam

April 14 had to come to an end, and it did. The excitement, pleasure, exhaustion and memories were all over. Whatever people could put up—meetings, gatherings, programmes, receptions—they had done.

'So everything is wrapped up,' Sushil called the next afternoon. 'Come over in the evening if you are free.'

It was an invitation to dinner. I knew that it would just be a time for drinking. I had no wish to go. Moreover, I was trying hard to not drink as often or as much. There was no reason behind this get-together. Thinking all this over, I said no.

'Aslam is sitting in my office,' Sushil said with a heavy voice. 'Listen to what he has to say.'

'Yes, brother.' Aslam's use of 'brother' and the way he said it meant that he wanted to ask me for a favour, for sure.

'How are you?'

'Not well. If someone could only help me out.' His voice held a request but also hesitation.

'What is it?' I got curious.

'That Ayesha, buddy.' He hesitated. His reluctance increased.

'What's happened to her?' I had trouble figuring out what he wanted to say.

'If you could only tell her once...' he managed to get out in spite of his reluctance.

'Am I a pimp for you?' I was suddenly agitated.

'Brother, you take offence so easily. One can't even speak one's mind to you. It's her profession after all...with me or with anyone else.'

Aslam was right. It was indeed her profession. How did it matter to Ayesha if it was Aslam or Kalra. Why did I feel so bad about it? Was I getting possessive about Ayesha? Was I afraid of seeing myself in the role of a pimp? Indeed, Aslam's request was a warning.

'If I can help you in this in any way, it's by giving you Kalra's number.'

Aslam showed some consideration too. Instead of arguing further, he took Kalra's number quietly. He had already met Kalra at the wedding. In any case, businessmen like Kalra understood the benefits of befriending a man like Sushil.

CHAPTER FIFTEEN

Ayesha, Back

'How are you?' Ayesha had returned from Nagpur after three or four days.

I had gone to Lucknow on university work. She had begun to call me on my mobile as soon as she returned, but I could not answer her calls because my phone was not on 'roaming'. Last month's bill of 2,500 rupees had sent my finances reeling, and to take 'roaming' calls would have flattened them totally. So while I wanted to talk to her, I couldn't. I called her as soon as I returned.

'I am not talking to you, Masterji,' she said sulking. I understood that she was actually angry but did not want to show it.

'How is Weber?' I tried to change the subject. I was a bit afraid of these emotional turns in our relationship. Was I in danger of weakening with her?

'Do you want to ask everything on the phone…don't you want to meet…see how dark I've become?' She blurted out everything together. 'Just come without a further word to Mandarin Fort at 7 pm; Weber will be with me.' She disconnected the call.

She did not wait for my yes or no. Maybe she guessed I would not be able to say no, which was correct because at 7 pm, I combed my hair neatly like an obedient child, and reached the place.

I looked around the restaurant. I was there for the first time. Ayesha's back was to the door but I recognised her. She was sitting alone at a table with her head bowed. She was filing her nails. I went up and stood before her. She did not even look up at me.

'Oh, you're here!' fell from her lips as I drew up a chair.

'Where's Weber?'

'Weber…yes, he…he's in the bathroom. He'll just be here.' She hesitated. 'How do I look, tell me?'

'Just as you were before.' In fact, I could find no change in her. But people who ask want to hear more than that.

'You're just saying that…See how dark I've become,' she said, stretching out both her arms.

I couldn't see any change in her arms either but to satisfy her, I grunted a 'Yes'. She was always worrying about her complexion. I had a sudden thought. Did she, after staying with Weber for four or five days, develop a greater consciousness about her fairness?

Then she kept talking about Mumbai, Puna, Sholapur, Nasik and Ratnagiri. She got carried away talking about the temple of Sai Baba at Shirdi. Then she broke down laughing that even the beggars there grow their beards and dress like Sai Baba when begging.

'Now, there of course, everyone was being very charitable. Masterji, is faith just a product of fear? Is it just fear that makes us do anything good? Is it fear that makes us afraid of God?' Ayesha threw a flurry of questions at me.

'Did you meet some writers there as well?' I avoided all her questions. I could not answer them for her. She had to figure them out herself, just as I had had to do for myself. These questions are doomed to be personal ones. No individual can answer them for another.

I had always regarded the authority of God and that of a mafia Don to be similar. This view would hardly be acceptable to Ayesha. She would have to find her own interpretation of the authority.

'Yes, I met writers…I could not bear it, listening to them… How they have survived hell. I used to think of myself as unfortunate…Weber was a good support.' Her face held an awkwardness at the mention of Weber.

I felt as if I had been to Mandarin Fort often, even though it was my first visit there. It looked like a model of European craft: a high ceiling resting on tall, white marble pillars in Roman style, benches strewn around in a park-like environment, besides the tables and chairs. Near the benches were plants in huge flowerpots. You could reach everywhere walking besides the railings, otherwise they acted like dividers. On one side was the bar and on the other, the coffee shop. The ice cream spot was further ahead. The bar had mirrors on all sides that let no one see inside, and everyone inside could watch the whole scene. There was a display board in the distance that gave the number serving toilets, pastry shop and ice cream parlour. Everything was quiet and organised. The Punjabi women in the chat corner were not making unnecessary noise either.

If you saw Mandarin Fort from the outside, as I had done many times, you could not guess at its glamour inside.

'Is Weber taking a shower in the bathroom?' I asked at the unnatural delay.

'No, he hasn't come. I was only joking with you,' she said neutrally, without raising her head. 'In fact, I did not invite him. One sword in one scabbard.'

I laughed. Partly at the sword-scabbard idea, and partly at her way of saying it. I was also pleased. I stretched out comfortably. Then I felt afraid, at my pleasure and relaxation.

It was getting dark outside. The entrance to the restaurant was at a 90-degree angle from where we sat. I looked up every time the door opened or closed. Other counters were all crowded, but we were the only ones at the bar.

'This place will get its crowd after 9 pm,' Ayesha told me, seeing that I kept looking at my watch. She told me that we'd get out of there at 9 because the spoilt children of rich parents would rule after that, with loud music and shouting that would rock the restaurant.

'Quarter to eight,' I looked at my watch when she said this. 'We have a full hour and a quarter.' We had both had a beer each.

'Did you meet Sushil?' I looked deep into her eyes, as deep as I could go.

I had wanted to ask her this as soon as I saw her, but had refrained. Had I come all the way just to ask this? I was wondering about that even when I left home.

'Yes, he called…' she met my eyes.

'Did you meet him as well?' my voice had something of curiosity and something of foreboding.

'Leave all this, Masterji,' she said softly and lowered her eyes.

She kept her eyes down as she sipped her beer.

Her open hair fell on her shoulders and partly, on her eyes. She had a dark suit with sparkles, and in the blue light of the restaurant…Ayesha sitting there sipping her beer was like a magical sight. After some time, she told me that Aslam had asked Kalra to have her meet Sushil at home. At that time, she had been in Pune. Kalra had called her that same evening in Pune. He was sitting with them when he called. She met him when she returned to Delhi. Kalra wanted her to go to them. 'I'll get your work done with the Police through B.N. Kaushik,' she had told Kalra. Kalra had responded with, 'Sushil is a scheduled caste, and S.C. officers do a lot for a small payment. They will pay you more as well because they have a caste inferiority complex.'

'So did Sushil, in fact, pay you more?' I was annoyed with Kalra. With that one sentence of his, he had made us all complicit in Sushil's behaviour.

'Weber is a good man, isn't he Masterji?' she asked, turning a deaf ear to my question. She kept sipping her beer quietly. The magic of the vision of a few minutes ago was gone.

We went back to our respective homes.

I understood that Weber had touched Ayesha's heart. I did not know much about Weber personally. I had trouble answering Ayesha's question and kept quiet. I had never met him before. We had always communicated by e-mails and only exchanged news, and that too about work and research. Anything personal only came up randomly. I knew that he was divorced twice, and had a child with each of his ex-wives. The children had been with their mothers, and were now in government custody.

I had faith that Ayesha would not misjudge a person. She had experienced trials from a very young age, and trials sharpen a person's perceptiveness.

I met Aslam and Sushil in the forthcoming days. I had wanted to know from them as well.

'What happened with Ayesha?' But both laughed away the question. I did not like their keeping the matter a secret.

'A horse cannot befriend the grass; what will he eat?' Kalra gave me this practical answer when I asked him. 'Why are you doing these investigations, Professor? Either be a saint or a sinner, don't play both games.'

Rana gave a hoot of laughter.

And indeed, I was myself mystified as to why I was doing these investigations.

CHAPTER SIXTEEN

Ayesha's New Life

'I have some disease, Masterji.'

It was the beginning of June. Summer was at its height. The heat had broken all previous records. The newspapers carried reports of people dying from the *loo*. They were, of course, all poor people. They must surely have been our people.

This was our first meeting after the restaurant in April. She kept phoning me but I kept making excuses to avoid her. I was trying to run away from her. She told me in a very pathetic way this time, 'You won't be able to recognise me.'

I went to her house on hearing this and, in fact, could not recognise her. There was no need to knock; the door was open. The house felt like a cemetery as soon as I stepped in, the same house that had blossomed with life. She had turned completely dark. Her eyes were sunk in their sockets and her face was swollen. Her golden hair had become like a dried bush. Her collarbones were sticking out. She was frightening, a female skeleton. I was scared and full of pity as well. I had thought that she was making up a story to get me over, and I had already prepared myself to scold her for the lie.

'Please sit…' her voice echoed from the depths.

'Has Weber?' The word in my mind escaped. Weber had returned to Germany the previous month, in May. I pulled a chair and sat down.

'I am so pitiable…I can't even get you a glass of water,' her voice echoed. She had either not heard me or chosen to seem she had not. She tried to get up but lost her breath.

'No, Ayesha, keep still. I am not thirsty.' I kept watching her.

Had it been Rana, Kalra, Sushil, and Aslam also? I knew well that Rana and Kalra did not use any preventive measures. My mouth felt dry. Ayesha had lain down, half-dead, again.

Was this the Ayesha that Sushil had been longing to hold in his arms? Was this the Ayesha that I had been questioning everyone about? Who was this corpse of an Ayesha, if not Ayesha herself?

'Jacqueline has gone to buy vegetables…let her come back…make some tea,' her broken voice echoed softly.

'What do the doctors say? Will it take 10 or 15 days more to recover?' I was worried. Did she have the disease I was thinking of, or was it just my prejudice?

She kept quiet, as if to prepare herself to answer. Her eyes were filling with tears. My guess was transforming into conviction. When I said 'What's happened, my brave girl?' she burst into tears.

'HIV,' she said, and her tears came running and would not stop. She was not loud even in her crying. She sobbed in a heart-rending way.

'It's a possibility...the blood sample has been sent...the report will come in a week...that is, the day after tomorrow... Masterji, in these four days I have seen Death.' Broken sentences fell out of her mouth between the sobs.

A small square of darkening sky was caught in a window behind Ayesha. Some dry branches of a tree were caught in the square as well. The room was filling up with darkness. I put on the tube light, which flickered twice, then filled the room with a sad, white light.

'When I wanted to die, Masterji, I could not. Now that I want to live, I am losing my life.' She gave a sob.

Her eyes kept filling with tears, then overflowing over her cheeks to lose themselves somewhere in her neck. I had not tried to hush her up.

'You will save my dead body from disgrace, won't you, Masterji? I have no one in this world apart from you,' tears were blurring her voice. 'You are unfortunate in this friend. I am leaving you with trouble even when I depart.'

My father's words came back to me. He always said that no one can live outside society. Even the Budhha, after becoming

'Buddha', had not stayed on in the jungles. He had, in fact, left them for society. No human being can turn their back on society. Yes, we each have the right to choose or make our society. Why had Ayesha not been able to do so?

'You are mad, my dear…nothing will happen to you…The disease is just suspected, not confirmed, right? Smile now…we need a mad young woman like you around,' I tried to control myself. I was overwrought as well. I went up to her and rested her head against my stomach.

'Save me!' She cried loudly now. 'I don't want to die…I want to live! Save me somehow, Masterji.' After crying for some time, she quietened down.

When the maid came, she asked her to make tea, then stopped her, 'He doesn't drink tea.' Her behaviour was strange.

'Make extra sweet tea for both of us,' I understood her suddenly.

'You are divine…' she folded her hands. Her face had a trace of happiness.

'Now what's my crime?' I returned to my chair. 'Don't try to abuse me…we are all humans.'

'Make tea for yourself too, Jacqueline,' Ayesha told her maid.

'Who is treating you?'

'Dr Taneja.'

'You should have gone to a government hospital or a big private hospital, not a little useless doctor,' I said with annoyance. 'He told you something and you believed it.' I had to raise her spirits somehow.

'I had fever the whole month. I was losing weight.'

'But that does not mean…Did you go to any other doctor?' I put my hand on her forehead.

'No,' She shook her head.

'Doctors make money by scaring their patients stiff. Theirs is also a business. It's a tricky world, you mad girl,' I had started scolding her. 'He must know about your work.' I looked at her as I asked her softly. I was conscious of Jacqueline's presence.

She nodded to say yes. 'I've been seeing him for years.'

'That's it…' I waved my hands in the air. I became convinced that I may be correct. I already saw that her disease was more of fear and stigma than a disease. 'You will come with me to a hospital. I'll have a check-up done by a good doctor.'

'No, I'll wait for the report.' She looked hurt.

Jacqueline arrived with the tea. She pulled up the table and put the cups on it. Then she went and sat with Ayesha on the bed. 'Is she in the same profession?' The harsh question came to my mind at her sitting so unhesitatingly. I scolded myself silently for the mean thought. After all, Ayesha could simply be giving her maid a lot of liberties. In spite of that, I was unable to keep myself from looking closely at Jacqueline's face, neck and breasts. Was that my love of beauty or my lust, or something else for which I have no name?

'You should go, didi. Certainty, even of disease, is better than suspicion.' Again, I felt as if Jacqueline knew something about it. I looked at Ayesha with a question. Ayesha shook her head 'no'. She understood the question.

The next day I brought her to the government hospital early in the morning. I knew a senior doctor there well. He cross-questioned Ayesha. Then he sent her to a junior doctor to give a blood sample for a test. 'Bring me a report in half an hour,' he told the doctor, who actually did bring a report back in half an hour.

'It's nothing. Typhoid gone bad, pneumonia as well.' Then he took and read the prescription Dr Taneja had given Ayesha.

'He definitely must have done his studies on a donation seat…the rascal.'

The next day, I myself went with Ayesha to Dr Taneja's clinic to pick up her report. The crowd outside extended well beyond the clinic. Working class people, and lower middle-class people and their relatives filled the benches to overflowing. We stood and waited our turn.

'Come in…come in Ayesha,' said a rotund Dr Taneja with fat cheeks. He had a thick gold chain around his neck, which looked more like a rope around a buffalo's neck. He wore a gold bracelet and big rings. 'How much gold does the man want?'

My mind filled with contempt for him. He showed no courtesy to Ayesha. His countenance had no respect for me either. For him, someone who came with a prostitute must be a pimp. 'Good news, dear…the test is negative. The goddess has been kind to you.' He put the report on the table.

Turning over the report, I felt like giving the doctor a good thrashing.

'S-l-a-p', the sound broke my thoughts. Ayesha had delivered a resounding slap on Dr Taneja's face. She was trembling with anger.

'You damn bitch…how dare you?!' Dr Taneja began to shake as well. He was as shocked as I was.

'Sit quietly on your seat doctor…I am Deputy Commissioner of Police, Sushil Kumar,' I said, taking Dr Taneja by the collar, and forced him down. It was necessary to tell this lie. The doctor looked pale.

'Let's go,' I said taking Ayesha's hand. 'Enough of him for now.'

The huge crowd in the clinic had fallen silent. It made way for us as we advanced. Ayesha had not been right to slap the doctor, but it was a small mistake compared to his own misconduct.

We reached home and I put her to bed. When I asked her why she had done that, she said tiredly, 'I don't know. Because of this man I was on death's door for four or five days.'

'Now what?'

The same square of sky was in the window but today it was full of radiance. The same dried branches were there but a couple of birds were chirruping there today.

'I want to leave this city.' She lay more comfortably. Her voice was still sad, but her face looked fresher.

'Then?'

'...'

'Why?'

'Everyone knows me here...I can't live in peace even if I try,' she said, her face expressionless.

'Meaning?' I was filled with curiosity.

'I won't be able to do this work any longer. You remember that fellow, Sevaram Shastri, who ran an NGO?' Her voice was still soft, without excitement. 'I called him three or four days ago and told him everything. I am surprised that he still wants to help me.' She stopped, out of breath. 'I want to go back to Kolkata,' she said after some time, her frail body livening a little with self-confidence.

'And work?'

'His NGO has a branch in Sonagachi.'

'I see.' Sonagachi was Kolkata's red light area—I knew this, but controlled my voice.

'I will work for prostitutes.'

It was strange hearing 'prostitute' from her mouth. Maybe she was mentally separating herself from that role. 'I will raise their consciousness…I will save them from this hell.'

'When do you want to go?' I felt a loneliness surround me.

'Could you not work right here in this city?' I gestured towards the largest red light district of the city.

She did not answer. We kept talking of this and that. Finally, we ran out of things to talk about. We sat together quietly for a long time. Jacqueline gave Ayesha some soup. She finished it all on my insistence. No one wants to eat when they are unwell…but it has to be done.

I was pleased at Ayesha's decision, but was sad at the prospect of her leaving to go away.

'Now you should leave,' Ayesha said to Jacqueline, handing the empty bowl.

'For where?' the words came out of my mouth.

'I can understand,' she smiled and looked better.

'I am hungry,' I said.

Ayesha told Jacqueline to cook some rice and dal immediately. She took out a wrap from the cupboard and asked me to change. I changed and sat down comfortably. Ayesha slid over to the other side of the double bed. She gestured to me to lie down on the bed. She moved her hand very slowly.

I reclined on the bed. A silence engulfed us. Jacqueline brought the food. I ate and went to sleep on the bed. Ayesha was already fast asleep.

She was completely well in a month. She did two things during this time. One, she sold her house and went to live on the other side of town in a rented house. Second, she changed her mobile number. She gave me the new number with the warning that I was not to give it to anyone without asking her.

I was pleased.

CHAPTER SEVENTEEN

Rana and Kalra

The days passed. Kalra, Sushil, Aslam and Rana each tried in their own ways to delve into her 'disappearance'. But even in the same city, it was impossible to get a clue about her whereabouts. Ayesha was clever enough. She spent most of her time at home; and when she had to go out, she wore a burqa, a full veil. She had rented her house as Mrs A. Khanum, whose husband was away earning in Dubai.

'Professor, it's not possible that Ayesha did not tell you where she is.' Kalra appeared with Rana at my doorstep one evening. They had been drinking, and started again as soon as they arrived. I was not surprised to hear him. They had understood my relationship with Ayesha by now.

'I went to meet her once when she was ill. I have not seen her since. She was talking of going back to her village.' I turned the conversation around. I had made a promise to Ayesha.

'No, she has not gone anywhere…and she is not ill any more,' Kalra said, gritting his teeth. 'You went to Dr Taneja with her, didn't you?' Kalra tried to search for the truth in my eyes.

'No!' I said with firmness.

'The last time some man went with her to the clinic…who called himself DCP Sushil Kumar,' he spoke as if to himself. 'Who could it be?'

I worried that he had come to me knowing fully well what had happened. In spite of that, I stuck to my decision that I would not tell them anything. Because, truthfully, had she not told me what she did, I would have been unknowing like them. I kept silent.

'Leave it, Kalra…if she's gone, she's gone. You have no dearth of others,' I looked at Rana, who was downing peg after peg. 'What do you say, Rana?'

'Exactly, sir!' he leaped at my question. 'Let her go to hell, Kalra, my friend. The damn bitch…whore…all of them are the same.' I realised that he was worse than Kalra.

'No, Professor, I have become habituated to Ayesha.' This was a less familiar side of the businesslike, pragmatic Kalra. It was a soft side.

'Leave it Kalra, my friend. What's attachment to a prostitute? Let's have the professor meet that film actress,' Rana said, glancing at me.

Now Kalra paid attention to finishing his drink. 'Have you heard that song, Professor…"my bodice is many-coloured, fill it with your own colours"?' he sang and then did a crude dance. Seeing him dance, I burst out laughing. Kalra laughed as well. Then he arose and joined Rana. Drinking had taken all the gravity out of a person. 'Jahnavi Goswami sang this song. Kalra had her over for Sushil.' Rana told the whole story. He was still dancing.

'Oh, we can't afford Jahnavi every day,' Kalra laughed. 'It costs 70-80,000 a night.' He sat down.

'But she's a delectable thing,' Rana added, as if slavering at the mouth.

Jahnavi Goswami had released two or three films recently. Before this, she used to work in TV serials. After the song 'my bodice is many-coloured' became a hit, she got many film roles with such songs.

Was this only one of her several professions? Had she reached it only through the means of selling her body? From a living woman she had become transformed into a thing, and people like Sushil, Kalra and Rana had become her customers...I was astounded.

'She too?' the words came out before I could stop them.

'Of course, my dear...the world has changed! It's work; it's a job...it may be dirty, but it's work...' Rana began to sing again.

'They have so many desires, how would they fulfil them all?' he said after a pause. He was making obscene gestures with his fingers.

'The heroine stops when her films run, and when the films stop, the heroine starts running,' Kalra said and held out his hand to Rana, at which Rana gave a high five on it. They were both beyond the pale.

'Call her once more, Kalra…show her to the professor.'

'Well?' Kalra looked at me and raised his eyebrows in a question.

'Rana, you think the professor is like you. You don't care for even your wife, you bastard,' Kalra said to Rana when I did not reply.

'Does my wife care for me?' Rana's voice had gone down. 'She was the one who started it.' He stopped dancing and sat down.

'What happened?' I was interested. I put my arm around Rana's neck.

'Professor, you have your head in books. Look at people like us. Our lives are in a ferment. Somehow, we keep a balance. I was transferred out for just two months and she couldn't wait for me.' His eyes were pitiable. He looked like a defeated soldier.

'Who was it?' I did start pitying him.

'It was a relative, the bastard. Didn't I have my needs too? Didn't I control myself? Are we such animals?' His pain increased.

'Could it be that you were misinformed?' I had known many cases like that.

In most cases, men begin to suspect their women on a simple piece of evidence and destroy their homes. They want to rule their women with an iron stick. If a woman so much as speaks to a man, they will imagine that it is a relationship. One man I know saw all this in his dreams. He saw his wife with one man or another in his dreams…and when he awoke, he fought with his wife. It was a disease that no psychoanalyst could cure, and certainly the poor woman could not.

'No…the whore admitted it, and said clearly "neither will I leave you nor can I live without him"', he began to scream.

'But why won't she leave you?' I was confused.

'She claimed that it was because the children's lives would get ruined, but the truth is that she has her eyes on my fat income and my house,' Rana's eyes were shining with anger and hatred as he said this.

I was taken aback. This world is indeed so unpredictable. At every step, we are presented with some unbelievable turn of the plot. 'My brother has gone through the same tragedy,' Kalra said. Apart from this, he said nothing before and after. He kept looking at nothing, wordlessly.

'Why don't you go to court and get a divorce?' I became agitated.

'She won't let me.' He paused. 'Cases based on a woman's infidelity keep dragging on in the court. They are impossible to prove.' He drank what remained in his glass in one gulp. 'I don't want to give her one paisa as alimony,' he was grinding his teeth in anger now. 'What does she want support for? Let her earn and survive. If I enjoyed her body, so did she enjoy mine.'

'I feel nauseous looking at her,' he replied, after thinking it over. My question had been, 'Do you still have physical relations?'

I was surprised even more at his answer. What made him feel nauseous once his wife had become intimate with someone else, and pay huge sums for prostitutes who had been intimate with hundreds of people?

I understood that there could be no re-establishing of trust between these two people. The best thing would be for them to voluntarily divorce. Otherwise, it was quite possible that one day there would be a murder or suicide. And the other person would waste his or her life in and out of court. The children, even if one parent was alive, would be like orphans, and have mental health problems. They would be afraid to get married, and if they did, would ruin one more family. If families were ruined, would the nation survive? Should divorce not be made simpler? When a man or a woman ceases to want to live with their man or woman, why does the other wish to continue tolerating insult and injury to stay on? I was like an insect caught in a spider's web with my net of questions, and they were strangling me.

A divorce was more in the interest of the woman than the man, no one could avoid seeing that. That a woman should say no to a divorce seemed to me the profoundest conspiracy of Manu's misogyny and male sexism.

'Rana, don't you have a shirt and pant of any other colour?' I tried to change the subject.

'I like this colour,' his voice still carried pain.

'Did you like to wear this right from childhood?' I was interested. I was pulled into a sociological analysis rather than a psychological one with his obsession with white.

'How could that be, Professor? We were not allowed to wear white in the village!'

The intensity of our earlier conversation was wearing off.

His answer confirmed my guess behind my question. His unusual love for white was a form of protest.

'Because of being poor?'

When I asked this, he began to laugh.

'You are born in the city, Professor. In the village, high caste people can break your backs with a stick. Brahmins may be poor as well, but they can wear white clothes. Why do people worship their feet? And why just the high caste, whoever has power rules the roost. Those who were Other Backward Castes till the other day, now behave in the same way with others. It's get kicked and, when you are in power, kick others. That's what the Jatav community is doing.'

'Do they oppress your caste in the village?' I was taken aback at what he said. All the non-Chamar castes were obsessed with this victimisation.

'They are certainly showing an attitude.' He had quietened down. I became quiet, too, to not push the topic too far. 'Give them fifty years of power and they will excel at it,' he ended bitterly.

Kalra was drinking away silently. He did not intervene even once, as if it was not his business, as if we were from different cultures.

'Have the Mahars in Maharashtra begun to oppress other Dalit castes?' I was saddened by his aloofness.

'I am not an educated man like you, Professor, but I know this much: the Mahars are in one state, and the Chamars are in all of North India. They will definitely come into power. We have no voice today ,and will have none tomorrow.'

He understood my ploy.

Was this his fear, or rivalry, or plain jealousy?

'And may I tell you that this political party of the Chamars will come to an understanding with the Brahmins again and again. After all, recognition can come only from the Brahmins. But the Brahmins do not like the Chamars, never have, and never will.

If they need someone, they will pick you or me…we are their natural allies, not the Chamars; they are each other's antagonists, and in this conflict the innocent Brahmins and innocent Chamars will suffer needlessly…' Rana delivered his speech in one breath.

Is this, in fact, the one political and social fact about India? I began to reflect on his statement, looking at recent past events.

Rana's opinions reeked of discontent. This discontent was anathema for mutual unity and struggle. There was an overall distrust of the Chamars on the part of non-Chamar castes. It was exactly like the distrust of the Mahars in Maharashtra by non-Mahar castes. Whose responsibility was it to turn this distrust into trust? The danger was that in this great war-strategy of Manu, if the smallest differences of identity began to matter so much, they would all fight and destroy each other.

Once upon a time, in the same way, the Nagas and the Garuds fought each other—fearful of, and provoked by, each other. Will all the smaller identities become vehicles for the Vishnus and gobble each other up? Was Rana forgetting that the vehicle receives only the whip and kick of the rider? Why had the Nagas not understood the pain of the Garuds…when they had been more capable of understanding?

The new Naga lineage should understand that the new Garud lineage could destroy democracy because of their resentment and frustration. Does anyone have the right to snatch away the identity of the Garuds and assimilate them in the Nagas? Can a hundred flowers not bloom? Will we stand by and watch while the Nagas, beloved vehicles of Shiva, are bitten by Vishnu's vehicle, the Garuds? Maybe our nation is doomed to bear all this until each of the different castes begin to feel empowered…

Finally, the two of them departed without getting a clue regarding Ayesha's whereabouts. I was forced to lie. It would have been suicidal for me to break her trust.

CHAPTER EIGHTEEN

Lalpur Khurd

'The village is called Lalpur Khurd,' Doctor Baney Singh folded his hands and produced a pitiable look in his eyes. 'And this is the Village Chief, his name is Bharatiram ji, sir….but everyone knows him as the Pradhan.' Bharatiram, the Pradhan, was shining, literally like the drops of moisture gathered on his sweaty skin, with the pride of being the Chief. He was looking at us with scorn.

It was the first week of September. The monsoons had been late this year, and were not over yet. There had been torrential rains in August. The dark clouds made it night in the middle of the day. The earth around had burst with unknown, unnameable plants.

In this season, I always remembered those childhood days when we would go off from our neighbourhood to search for plants by the rivulet. The city was different then. There was one road, on which trucks would sometimes pass. We were instructed to never go on the road; to cross the road was to venture very far, for us. We would venture far…to search for plants in the rains, for newborn puppies in winter, for empty matchboxes to play with, for asking for 'Lohri' at the festival, and for a hidden puff of a cigarette.

We friends had decided to meet in May, but one or the other of us was always busy. We had, at most, managed to sit down once or twice to talk. Then all the work descended on me. As far as officers were concerned, a teacher's time had no value. A teacher was free, and an officer was preoccupied with big, important work. They had money, I supposedly had time… they certainly had no time. We were all donating what we had.

Meanwhile, we had registered a non-government organisation called 'Sanghamitra'. The area we had earmarked for our work was in the heart of the city but seemed as if it was in a faraway jungle. It was the residence of 747 families in the Forest Zone of the metropolis. The families had been living there for 30 or 40 years but had no ownership rights —nor could they get any. This was a protected Forest Zone under the district and forest authorities, and residence was strictly forbidden. The land could not be sold or purchased, although when the families had come to live there, it had not yet been declared 'Protected'. Now it was the fault of these poor and helpless people that they had no rights.

The families had left Rajasthan for the city. They would labour the whole day at a construction site, and sleep by the wayside at night. Gradually, some wise and courageous people among them had persuaded and paid the village's Jats to let them camp there. Then it slowly became a regular neighbourhood—first Lalsinghpur, after the name of the first Chief, then just Lalpur Khurd. Because there were villages around, people began to call it Village Lalpur Khurd.

It had not been easy to find Lalpur Khurd. I would not have found it either, had Rajbir not been my student. Rajbir was from Rajpur Khurd, a neighbouring village. He was the first and only young man to have reached university from his village.

Rajbir showed me the village. He took me around and introduced me to Dr Baney Singh. Baney Singh was a Sikh, and carried out his medical practice in the village. He was actually a compounder, and assisted the doctor in Rajbir's village. That doctor had himself been a compounder. Baney Singh, like him, learnt to be a doctor from watching the doctor as a compounder. Compounder Baney Singh had a Red Cross on one side and a picture of Guru Nanak on the other, on which was written in small letters 'Prayers and Medicine are Both Essential'.

'Sir ji, everyone in this village is a tuberculosis patient… you should not bother to come here,' Dr Baney Singh told me. His small and loose top knot would shake as he talked. This was at our first meeting.

It was the last days of June. The village was breathing fire even at six in the evening. There were little hillocks of yellow sand as far as the eye could see, full of dry bushes. I had asked what were the main medical problems of the villagers, to which this was his response. I went again a few times but by chance had never managed to meet the village chief. Then, the rains in August not only made a visit difficult but impossible.

It was I who had to decide which the village needed more, a dispensary or a school. Because it was forest land, we were not permitted to build a permanent structure there. We had all gathered to discuss these things when Dr Baney Singh brought the Pradhan.

'Pradhanji, what are your main problems?' Jayant forged ahead. He had taken the lead in asking questions so far, eliciting the village chief's name and introduction.

'Tell me what you can do for us…We have a thousand problems,' Pradhan Bharatiram said, his attitude full of scorn.

'Look here, Pradhanji, we can only do something once we know what needs to be done,' Firoz read the annoyance on Jayant's face and took over. An officer was not accustomed to hearing a question in response to his own question.

'Then why do you bother to do anything at all?' he said, taking out a packet of *bidis* from his pocket and puffing away rudely.

That was his brief answer to Firoz.

We looked at each other with questioning eyes. Now what? The Pradhan was certainly older than us, but his behaviour was not only beyond our comprehension, it was very annoying. Over fifty in age, he was short and weak looking, wearing a white kurta-pyjama. His scornful attitude puzzled us and left us with nothing to say.

Firoz and Jayant's faces showed defeat.

'Pradhan ji, stop doing your politics, and tell them what you have on your mind,' Rajbir scolded him in their local language. 'The DCP sahib is sitting in front of you,' he added, pointing at Sushil.

'No, no, that's nothing. Don't be afraid. If you don't want us to work here, never mind.' Sushil spoke very courteously, and looked at me to say, 'We can locate another place, can't we?'

I liked Sushil's style.

The Pradhan's face had become further twisted with pride and scorn on hearing Rajbir's words. Now Sushil's gentle tones were a warning. The tea arrived. While we drank tea, we avoided all mention of the village and our organisation. The Pradhan was unable to take part in our conversation at all.

'All right then, Pradhanji,' Sushil said, arising. Everyone was done with their tea.

'So long, Pardhanji.' Dr Baney Singh also arose.

'One minute, sir, wait…What do you want to do…I'd be grateful if you could explain your purposes.' This time he had request in his eyes.

The Pradhan, it turned out, was a once bitten twice shy man. We told him in detail about our organisation and our purposes. We also shared our doubts, difficulties and limitations with him. Among these were caste, a shortage of funds and being tied up to government jobs.

'You are our own people,' he blurted out on hearing about the caste. Then he told us his previous experiences when NGO workers had come to the neighbourhood two or three times before. They had made some girls pregnant and run away. They had received a lot of funding and not spent any in the village. All this talk was good for building up our mutual trust.

'This village has a tuberculosis epidemic. There is a patient in almost every house,' the Pradhan told us. 'Come to my house and you will see that I keep DDT powder sprinkled all around.' Dr Baney Singh had shown me his house. Indeed, the powder was a protective armour all around his house. 'But the biggest problem is of water. We get water, but it is so yellow and stinky that you cannot drink it.' This was the situation in the heart of a metropolis. Rajbir was taking notes.

'Could we go to the village right now?' Sushil looked at the clock, which showed 4 pm.

'Why not?' said Dr Baney Singh promptly. 'It's only 15 minutes away.'

Then we went in a motorcade of our three cars to the village. From a main road of the city, the car had to go some one-and-a-half kilometres inside. I had passed the bend on that main road a thousand times but until June, I had no idea of the world inside. It was indeed another world. Huge boulders and small hillocks were surrounded by bushes and dust. A man hiding just 20 feet away could be invisible. The recent rains had made puddles on the road.

At the mouth of the village was a tea and cigarette shop. A few people sat there looking around at nothing. There were 10 stray dogs in the place, of which a few were stretched out sleeping in the middle of the road. Others were chasing each other around. On hearing the cars, men and dogs both stirred themselves and started looking at us. One or two of both men and dogs showed unusual enthusiasm and started barking or talking. All the rest kept staring steadfastly.

'Ram-Ram Pardhan ji,' a few greeted Bharatiram as he descended from the car.

The Pradhan's attitude was no less than a national politician's. As soon as we entered the settlement, our eyes fell on a man lying in the middle of the road.

Seeing the question in our eyes, Baney Singh said, 'No, sir, he is drunk.' 'Ramcharan,' the Pradhan tried to shake the man awake but he kept sleeping. Then Baney Singh and the Pradhan pulled him to one side and laid him under the neem tree.

'Alcohol is another thing that's ruined them. But if they don't drink, they would go crazy and die. They get work for three days and are useless for the others.' The Pradhan acted as if he was delivering a speech.

This kind of argument in defence of drinking always irritates me. Men have come up with different arguments to defend drinking. Do women then die from not drinking when they face the same problems? They continue to live and to run their households. In front of us, groups of men were busy playing cards. Was there the same explanation for playing cards? I was surprised that we had not seen a woman so far. It was a world of men, devoid of women.

The settlement was not unclean; if anything, it was overly clean. I noticed this in every lane we passed. The sound of crying and lamenting came from a distance. We looked at the Pradhan. In answer, he led us in this direction.

'She died during childbirth, sir.' Dr Baney Singh talked to the men standing there and came back to tell us.

'Was she unmarried?' asked Jayant.

'No, sir, she had three or four children,' answered a man from the group who came and stood with us.

'Come on, let's go ahead…these are Chamar homes,' Dr Baney Singh muttered as we forged ahead. We had hardly begun to figure out what he might be implying when there was a sudden disturbance on the road. Children began running forward, holding plastic cans. They were heading towards a crossing, the same where groups were playing cards. Women were also taking fast strides to get there. Now the deathbed had only some men near it.

'It must be the water tanker. It comes once in three days.' The Pradhan seemed a bit lost in his thoughts. 'One does need water.'

'What are the other castes in the village?' Sushil put his hand on Dr Baney Singh's shoulder. We had grasped so far that Dr Baney Singh was not a Chamar. The drain near the deathbed was swarming with flies.

'There are Balais, Nais, Dhobis, Muslims…all the castes, sir,' Dr Baney Singh replied, walking on.

'Which one is in the majority?'

'We are, sir.' Dr Baney Singh saw the question in our eyes. 'The Balais,' he clarified.

Is that why Bharatiram was the village Chief? Was that why the water tanker came to the Balai quarter? Was that why the Balai men were engrossed with their cards even when a young person had just died in their midst? It was not their business, it seemed.

'And Valmikis?' Sushil asked Dr Baney Singh.

'You mean Harijans? Yes, Harijans have their homes on the other side of the village…they have some 30 or 40 homes,' the Pradhan answered this time, perhaps because he wanted to save his reducing importance. 'They have less to do with the village.'

Sushil's face had hardened on hearing the Pradhan's words but he kept quiet.

'And Khatiks?' I found myself asking. I was myself surprised at my question…why had I asked?

'Yes, sir, the Khatiks also have six or seven homes,' the Pradhan answered. 'The Jats have two homes, the Muslims have three.'

'Is there a government school here?' Jayant asked. Four or five starving children had joined us.

'There is a Primary School here. There is a Higher Secondary School in Rajpur Khurd, but it is far…children hardly manage to go to the Primary School.'

'Why not?' we all asked together in one voice, then looked at each other and smiled.

'The men and women both go to work. The older children stay back at home to look after the younger ones. If the older ones were to go to school, who would look after the younger ones?' he answered very simply.

Turning around in the lanes, we had reached the houses of

the Valmikis. Maybe one of us had asked the Pradhan to take us there.

'How many boys are 10th pass?' asked Firoz.

'Two,' replied Baney Singh.

'And girls?' asked Jayant.

'There's not a single one, sir. Girls don't go to school any longer,' the Pradhan said in a dead voice, and looked at Baney Singh in a mysterious way.

'Why not? Education is even more important for girls,' Sushil said in an advisory tone. A child who had polio was standing close to him.

'You're right. But we are helpless,' Baney Singh said, looking at Rajbir. Then he chased the child away.

Rajbir understood the unspoken message. He started to narrate how a girl from the village had scored the highest marks in the Class 10 Board Exam. Her name was Priyanka Kapoor. She was a Balai by caste and her father was a mason. Since the school was in Rajpur Khurd, she had to walk a distance to reach it. Priyanka was attractive to look at. The teacher Ramratan Sharma at Rajpur Khurd was especially fond of her. He taught her extra after school. There were three reasons for that. One was that his wife could not have children, and there was no longer any chance of having any. The second was that the Sharmas were from Jaipur in Rajasthan, the same place as Priyanka's father Badluram. Third, Badluram had built the teacher's house for a modest payment. Meanwhile, Dhaniram, son of another villager called Ratiram, fell in love with the girl. He would harass her whenever possible.

The teacher, upon Priyanka's complaints, warned Ratiram about his son's behaviour.

Ratiram took action on the teacher's complaints, and had Dhaniram beaten in the middle of the bazaar and apologise to Priyanka as a sister. Ratiram was a simple, honest man. He took a beating to be the solution of every problem. Dhaniram took revenge on his father through Priyanka. When she was returning from school, she was attacked by seven or eight Jat boys, raped and killed.

We were stunned to hear this story from Rajbir. What kind of world did we live in?

'And Dhaniram?' Jayant burst out.

'Oh, what could ever happen to him? Ratiram paid off the police. He said the girl is dead now, why kill the boy too?' the Pradhan's hollow voice matched his hollowed-out body. 'What a girl she was…a diamond. I used to call her "Nagina" in affection,' his eyes overflowed with love as he said this. 'She had "Dictation" in all five subjects,' he said, meaning 'Distinction'. 'She did not have less than 80 marks in any subject,' his voice was proud. 'We are stuck between a rock and a hard place,' he finished with pain in his voice.

'We'll come at 10 in the morning next week,' we told the Pradhan while leaving.

The next week, we went there with a group of doctors and did a preliminary testing. After running around for over a month, we managed to get a water pipeline to the village.

'Break up this caste discrimination between you all, Pradhan ji,' Sushil said. Sushil had understood that the Pradhan, being a Balai, considered himself higher than other castes. The Pradhan had mentioned often that 'we' were higher than the Chamars. We don't skin leather, we weave cloth.

'But in Ajmer, the Balais make shoes,' I said, aiming wildly at a target.

'Well, we are from Jaipur. We don't inter-dine or inter-marry with those other people,' he replied stiffly. 'Ours is only the cloth work. We have Gandhi, Kapoor and Khurana in our caste.'

'So those others are not Balais?' asked Jayant.

'No, they are Balais, but not our kind of Balais. They are different.'

'Meaning lower?' Jayant asked again.

'Yes, sir, that's right. Lower.' The Pradhan's attitude had pride, superiority, scorn.

'So, you are a Koli?' I pressed the Pradhan.

'No, sir, Kolis are different. We have nothing to do with the Kolis,' Dr Baney Singh interrupted. 'For example, my full name is Dr Baney Singh Khurana. The Pradhan's name is Bharatiram Gandhi. Our subcaste is separate from the Kolis,' he tried to clarify.

'There must be many Khuranas in this neighbourhood,' I said deliberately to Baney Singh.

'Not at all, sir. The majority are the Gandhis. We are only 50 or 60 families, that's all,' Baney Singh sounded disappointed and frustrated.

So, was Bharatiram the chief only because his caste ruled with three or four hundred families? I couldn't help but think that. Meanwhile, we had made up our minds that the most dire needs were for a crèche and a primary health clinic. About 20 women had joined our group; the group kept expanding. So was our self-confidence expanding. Dr Sukhdev Singh Tanwar, the local Jat member of the Legislative Assembly, joined us as well.

CHAPTER NINETEEN

Ayesha Finally Leaves

Ayesha phoned on Friday evening, and after talking about this and that, asked, 'Can you meet on Sunday, Masterji?'

It was the first week of October. On my agreeing, she called me to St Paul's Missionary Church to meet. I reached exactly at 1:30 as she wanted. She and Jacqueline had just emerged from their prayers. 'You go home,' she told Jacqueline as they neared me.

Jacqueline came up to me and said 'Hello sir'. Though she did not have a fair complexion, she looked radiant in a dark blue top. She could have been around 35 or 36 years old. Ayesha had told me that she was from Agra, and the victim of many misfortunes. Was she a Dalit? The thought teased me on looking at her.

'Masterji!' Ayesha's voice broke the spell. She was smiling, and asked 'What's the matter?' in an insinuating way. I was myself startled to find that, unlike myself, I was staring away at Jacqueline. Then she left, and we went and sat in the park next to the church.

The weather was pleasant. The sun was not strong, but it couldn't be tolerated for too long either. We sat on the bench under the Gulmohar tree. The sunlight fell on us in specks, spreading over Ayesha's whole body like leaves.

'I am leaving on the 7th, that is, in two days,' she said without looking at me. In front of her were people cutting grass. Her voice was peaceful, as was the grass standing in the shade.The gardener was fixing the lawn mower. He would fiddle with the wire, then with the container for collecting the grass. After some trouble, he got it right.

'I've been there two or three times now. Sevaramji is not a bad person. His wife died long ago. He did not re-marry for his children's sake. Now he is alone, after they have grown up and left home,' Ayesha told me calmly about Sevaram Shastri.

The gardener had started mowing. The roaring of the machine filled the air. He would go in a straight line, then turn and come back. The grass was collecting in the container.

'You will live with him now?' I asked in a calm voice.

'I am not going to leap from the frying pan into the fire, Masterji.' She understood what I was getting at. The gardener had stopped his mowing and there was a sudden silence all around. 'I have seen the area. It's a virtual hell on earth. I was particularly ashamed because I am a Bengali. Sonagachhi is a blight on the fair face of Kolkata.'

She proceeded to tell me about her travels and meetings with people there. She told me in detail, upon my asking, about the office there. She told me about her many plans. She had also met Sangita many times, and had said many things to her in my favour. She had not told Sangita the truth about herself. She had stopped Sangita many times from having an abortion.

'Weber has reached there,' Ayesha informed me. I was stunned that he had not told me about his coming to India.

'We will work together for some time. He is a good man, isn't he, Masterji?' It was phrased as a question, but it didn't seem to be a question to me. At best, it was a request for confirmation. I didn't feel up to confirming it.

The gardener had finished his mowing, and was now busy opening the container. Two figures that looked like village women were trying to stuff the bundles of grass into their sacks. 'Fill it, fill it up tight…don't leave any outside. Open it up well, stuff it all inside.' The gardener was using inuendoes and speaking obscenely, and the two women, unaware, were indeed opening their sacks wide and stuffing the grass in.

'He has feelings for me,' Ayesha clarified, maybe because I was quiet. Ayesha's attention was not on the gardener. She had not even heard his words.

'And what about you?' I was on both sides. Maybe it was my pleasure, or my pain, or simply my policy.

'Me?' A smile slowly spread over her face. 'You yourself are not interested in me; I know.' She kept looking at the setting sun which was now behind the dome of the church, and only its rays were visible from behind, as if to announce that it was there but as good as not there. 'If I could be with you…but…you…!'

She wanted to say something but both her tongue and her brain were not helping her out.

'Weber knows about you?' I could not forget, no matter how hard I tried, that she had a profession that was considered wrong in polite society.

'There is no need for that between us,' her tone was sharp.

'Meaning?' Her tone had hurt me—its lack of clarity as much as its sharpness.

'He did not ask, and I did not tell.' She was looking out into the distance again.

'No one can have feelings after knowing all that about my past. I am going to bury my past right here and leave.'

Her brows were knitted but her voice stayed calm.

'But your past…may be a problem for him.' I thought of the past at times as a mad dog that, once it started chasing you, did not leave you no matter what. I was myself exhausted from the chase of this mad dog.

'Is that what makes you afraid of me, Masterji?' Ayesha held my chin and turned it towards her. She tried to look into my eyes for the truth. I was uncomfortable by her direct question, but managed to hide it.

I had no doubt started liking Ayesha. She was beautiful, of course, but she was also wise. Her common sense was well developed. I never felt that we could not understand each other when we talked. She had begun to fathom my gestures and expressions as well as my speech. There was more intimacy, depth and attraction between us than for me with anyone else. Yet, in spite of that, she could not have taken Sangita's place. Was she correct in her question then?

We kept circling the ring, the question between us. A silence descended on us, together with the evening. We were in its twilight, close to each other as well as far. I could not decide what to say next.

I had always tried to avoid unnecessary lies and pretense. Without wanting to, in the lovely silence of the evening, my hand went unplanned to her shoulders. I did not want it… but…there was no one now, except us. The gardener and the village women had left ages back.

There was the cool shadow of the church. There was the indifference of Sangita. The warmth of our bodies.

My other hand raised her face to mine. Her eyes looked into mine for a moment, then were lowered, were raised again, and lowered again, and remained closed. It was a silent invitation. The innocence of the eyes had spread over her face, to her nose and her lips.

I told myself…no.

But in that same split second my lips were glued to hers. Her fingers were entwined in mine. They were trembling, together with her breasts. My breathing was fast, like a furnace, and hot as well.

We came apart for a minute. Her eyes had a strange invitation, wild and abandoned. Then she put her mouth on mine again, as if to suck an ice candy like a child.

This was the first gift we had given each other after a year of friendship. Maybe I did not want all this, but I had not been able to stop her, or myself.

I knew she was a prostitute, but she was no longer one. She had left the work. In any case, she had never been a prostitute for me but simply a friend. It was a relationship outside all the defined ones in society. I had never regarded her as a 'thing' but had created a relationship with her. We stayed thus, entwined, for a long time, unaware of our surroundings. I thought about us, holding her to me. She must have needed me after her illness. As for me, I had been indisposed myself for seven months. I kept trying to justify my behaviour.

She invited me for beer for the last time that evening. On my asking 'Why?', she said, 'I want to keep this memory as a special one all my life.' She held my hands in her own soft, warm ones. We went home…not the Big Banana…not Mandarin Fort. I bought cold beer on the way, that she insisted on paying for. At least this time I tried to pay but she would not let me.

Were these anything but foolish, sentimental moments? But how pleasurable such foolish, sentimental moments could be.

'Jacqueline, please leave,' Ayesha requested her as soon as we reached her place, holding her wrist.

'Where will she go? She stays here, doesn't she?' I asked.

'My brother's place,' Jacqueline answered promptly.

Jacqueline asked about dinner, and we both looked at each other. She entered the kitchen. First, she brought 3 glasses and put them on the table.

'3 glasses?' asked my eyes.

'For Jacqueline,' Ayesha smiled.

'A good democratic system,' I laughed.

I started taking out the bottles, packets and other things from the bag. Ayesha arranged the glasses and brought the bottle opener. I poured the beer equally in the glasses. Meanwhile, Jacqueline brought a plate of green salad, and unhesitatingly picked up a glass and took it back with her. She said 'thanks' as she took it. There was the smell of rice and spices, and the rattle of dishes from the kitchen.

'What will I do after you leave?' I said as we sat quietly drinking—as when you have nothing left to say when you say goodbye to a close person. But were we actually quiet? Or quietly waiting for something to happen? Or preparing ourselves for some special momentous turn of events? She did not answer my question.

We kept lifting and putting down our glasses. A spider had woven its web of silence around us. There was nothing for us outside, and inside was only our breath. Jacqueline had entered the web a few times but had not disturbed us. 'Rice and egg curry' were her words that she dropped inside the web.

'Can I watch TV in the other room?' Jacqueline had asked but did not wait for an answer. Ayesha said neither a yes nor a no. Jacqueline comfortably picked up the remaining half bottle and her glass, then came back and took a plate of food from the kitchen. Soon, there was the echo of loud voices from the next room.

I spent the night there and came home the next morning. Jacqueline watched TV till late, then fell asleep on the sofa, with the lights and TV on. I felt refreshed when I woke up in the morning. Ayesha was still sleeping, her eyes partly open and moving. 'Is she having a dream?' I wondered.

Ayesha left three days later. She had found her purpose in life, and was very happy to have done so. In her happy state, she could only spread happiness all around.

Weber stayed with Ayesha. He went back to Germany a few times, but returned to settle down here. On his insistence, Ayesha learnt some meditation in the Osho commune in Pune under 'Bhagwan' Rajneesh, and began to work with Weber to run the camp in Sonagachhi.

Their organisation 'Before Awakening' that worked for AIDS awareness even hosted Bill Clinton once.

Weber and Ayesha did not marry but they came to have a huge family.

CHAPTER TWENTY

Sangita Says No

The next time I saw Sangita after Rinku's wedding was from a bus as I was passing by. She was walking on the footpath with a woman, and I was in the bus. Her stomach was big. She had gone back with Sudesh chacha and Sukhjot chachi after the wedding. She had not listened to Amma and Papa's entreaties to stay on. She was such a decisive person that I had been unable to gather the courage to approach her. I knew she would not stay ,and did not wish to be insulted by asking her.

It was afternoon. The sun was quite hot. The bus was already an oven with its tin roof; the tarred road was no less. I felt engulfed by flames as I got down from the bus. I could not stand the hot sun. Jayant and Firoz laughed at this sensitivity of mine. 'And you are from Rajasthan!' It was the sort of humour that made people make fun of me saying, 'And you a Dalit!'

The loo was pounding its heat around. The bus and the road were both almost empty. They approached slowly. First, I could see their black umbrellas, then their faces, then the rest of them. I was alone at the bus stop, waiting. In spite of the shade of the bus stop, I was breathing heavily.

'Jai Bhim, Prerna ji.' I now recognised the woman with Sangita. She was the head nurse in the dispensary. I had turned my back so far so that they would not recognise me till I was ready. There was no trusting Sangita. She would have changed her course.

After Rinku's wedding, I tried to call on her mobile every week, and indeed at first, three or four times a day. Her mobile would keep ringing and she would not pick up. Then when she began to disconnect it, I cooled down a little. Once in a while I tried calling her from unknown numbers. She would stay silent after hearing my 'Hello', or silently cut it off. I'd keep saying what I had to say.

Had the fear of Ayesha not been enough of a fear?

'Jai Bhim ji, jai Bhim, namo Budhhay,' Prerna went on ahead, panting. She knew our affairs well. Sangita was also panting. Her mouth was open like a bird's beak.

'I have to say something,' I could not contain myself, as Sangita too tried to move ahead. She looked indifferent. She paused for a moment and looked at me questioningly. Her look was hostile…it had nothing but indifference. But she had stopped.

'Go ahead,' she told Prerna.

The back did not react. It did not turn around. It had heard, and Prerna kept walking on, as if she already knew of everything happening. Sangita had saved me from being insulted in front of Prerna. She had become a careful enemy.

'Speak,' she said, putting her hand for support on the railing of the bus stop but removing it immediately, perhaps because it was too hot. 'It's very hot.' The words fell from her mouth like three drops of steam.

'Yes.' I nodded.

'You are here in this heat…' she managed to say the complete thought in an incomplete sentence.

Has she felt worried for me? Had she said it sarcastically? Was it just a courteous question? The questions burst into my mind all together.

'My life without you…' I was unable to complete my sentence as well. She could have considered it hypocritical, which would have hurt me. Unreciprocated feelings have to be controlled, no matter what the goodwill on the other side. Is this civilisation? Is this wisdom? If indeed it is civilisation and wisdom, why must we have it?

She seemed to take my half-sentence for a complete one. She cast her eyes down.

We stood there baking for some time on the hot road in the cast-iron bus stop. Then we got into an auto rickshaw without a comment to the auto rickshaw driver for asking for too high a fare. She wanted to go home and I, to a restaurant. She won. She kept the auto rickshaw going around pointlessly for half an hour but would not accept my idea of going to a restaurant. I had asked her to come back to me. At first, she gave no answer. She kept changing the subject but upon my insistence she gave a brief 'No' in answer.

'What should I do?' I asked in a dead voice.

'Marry Ayesha.' She was looking at the golden sunlight that was throwing a golden light on her face.

'She's a good girl…she came to see me a few times recently. She loves you.'

'How do you know?' I was annoyed.

'I know you,' she lashed out at me again. 'You want to commit the sin but you want to be safe from it too.'

Was she, in fact, explaining to me the very conundrum I had been unable to figure out, or because of my wiliness, did not wish to figure out?

'Right, right, that's how I am…why not? I want to taste the forbidden fruit and be safe as well. Not that I did not have scores of secret occasions to taste the fruit without anyone knowing…I had many such, but I chose not to use them.'

Did I want to raise myself in my own eyes? Did some kind of conscience have control over me? Was I suspended somewhere between my desires and my upbringing? Was I afraid of someone? Definitely, there was something that stopped me from being reckless. There was something that made me aware of my buried desires, but stopped them from bursting into life. This something made me neither live, nor die. I could find neither Paradise, nor its angels. I could find neither Hell, nor its fire.

Sangita had found an entrance to my dark dungeons, where I had been blindly and unknowingly feeling around to identify different, separate things.

'What are you trying to say?' I again acted uncomprehending.

'Just that you must have first tried to attract her to yourself, and then you must have retreated.'

I was relieved to hear what she thought—it was nothing like I had feared.

Her one statement, however, had explained me to myself. 'Horrible' was the word that came to my mind. It referred to me, or to my mistaken pleasure in escaping without sin, or to my overall stupidity.

'You imagine all kinds of things. Don't make the mistake of thinking yourself all-wise by accusing me of whatever you like,' I counter-attacked.

The power of a woman seemed to lie in their control of slave-like men. I couldn't forget this if I tried. I couldn't forget those homes where women exercised such control. They were not homes, they were pits of conflict.

'Am I a male chauvinist?' I was worried. I was only afraid of my memories. I only wanted to run my family, save my home. But nothing had remained…no home…no family… no life.

Was it not the inability of men to accept women's strength that had made pits of conflict out of the homes where women ruled? Didn't upper castes have the same problem with the intelligence and strength of Dalits and lower castes? Didn't America show the same intolerance towards Third World nations?

Which is why such families, nations, and the whole world had become pits of conflict.

'I have made everything clear to Ayesha. I don't want to talk about it anymore.' Her attitude was so cut and dried that I did not have the courage to bring it up again.

'I love you very much, Sangita.'

I did mean it, but there was also a shadow of a thought that the strongest women become weak upon the voluntary surrender of men.

Again, the analogy occurred to me: otherwise strong Dalits and Other Backward Classes are also weakened by the false surrender of upper castes. Does this false surrender not fool them into believing that their power is now accepted? Doesn't some feeling of inferiority destroy their identity? What a turnaround!

'It's possible,' she said, taking her hand away from mine, which I had taken and was holding. 'There's no meaning to all this anymore.'

These were heavy words, though her voice was light-hearted. I found myself buried under the weight of the words. 'Stay happy where you are, and I will stay happy in myself.'

'This baby needs me as much as it needs you,' I said putting my hand on her extended belly.

There was no wile in this statement, only love and responsibility. The baby was not hers, it was not mine. It belonged to both of us. It was the meaning of our existence. It was the product of our existence. It was the future of our present.

'Sometimes I wonder why I am alive,' she whispered. 'I have a hundred reasons to die, not a single one to live, yet I don't die. Why? The only reason is that I am producing something. That gives me the motive to live. There is nothing beyond, but here, now, is this. I am also afraid…of loneliness, of myself, of you… but there's nothing I can do.'

She kept talking in fits and starts, just like the sunlight that fell all around us, in spite of the black rexine covers on the sides of the auto.

'Life is given only once. Marriage is just a prop like many others. A prop to overcome and share solitude.' Her eyes looked into the distance. 'The body finds its own paths.'

'Come back, please.' I folded both hands in front of her. She turned her face and looked outside.

I was suddenly aware of the auto driver's presence. He was preoccupied with his driving, his eyes on the shining sunlit road outside. He had understood that it was a husband-wife quarrel, and that we needed all the time we could get. He was driving at his whim. He turned wherever he wanted, and parked under any clump of trees on the pretext of relieving himself. He had already relieved himself twice and bought cigarettes twice. He was a decent man, but our attention was elsewhere. We were in another world, and this world had no meaning for us.

'I am only following Amma and Ayesha's advice because the baby is innocent and should not be punished,' she said after a few moments' silence.

'I don't want to feel guilty like you in front of this innocent being…nothing more than that….those who dream big also fall big.'

I dropped her at her hostel gates.

'Madam will come back, sir.' With a lower-class sentimentality, the auto driver had chosen to interfere. I was not in a state to respond.

I had to try especially hard to fall asleep that night. The same things would go round and round, and come back to me from different directions. I was haunted by the things I had not been able to say. I was angry about the things I had forgotten to say. I was exhausted by the new angles opening to all these things. I searched for the sleep that had vanished somewhere. I tried sleeping on the left side, then the right. I put my right hand on my chest, then my left one. Sometimes I made a fist of both hands and put that on my stomach. I lay flat on my back. I lay on my stomach. But sleep refused to come.

I sat up, then lay down, then got up again, and began to walk up and down the room. The things in my head would not let me go and sleep was eluding me. I did this on other nights as well but then some new thought would show me a ray of hope and allow me to sink into sleep. This night was different.

I once heard from Sukhjot chachi that Sangita had had a showdown with a colleague in the dispensary. I wanted to know the details but chachi kept avoiding the subject. Usually, I did not insist if someone hesitated to tell me something. But this concerned Sangita and what concerned her, concerned me. After a lot of fussing, what she told me left me shocked. I was angry, but more than that, I was frustrated.

The colleague was a doctor called Aditya. He was unmarried and liked Sangita. He liked to declare his love to Sangita even after her forbidding him to, many times. Maybe Sangita's leaving me had filled Aditya with hope, just as Firoz had developed hopes about Nigar.

'I'll knock that son of a bitch's teeth out,' I called Sangita that evening to say. I said many other extreme things. I had lost control over myself.

'Who are you to meddle?' she finally broke her silence. 'This is my life...Mind your own business.' This was such a bitter and uncaring attitude that I found it hard to believe that this was my old Sangita speaking. Her tone had made me lose my whole bearing on the world.

'But there is still something between us.' These words did not come out themselves. They were like heavy stones that had to be forcefully pushed out.

'No, that is a misconception...This is solely my affair,' Sangita said, and disconnected the phone.

'Do you talk to her sometimes?' I went to meet Amma. It was a rainy day. In spite of an umbrella, I had got drenched.

'Yes,' Amma said, half-lying on her bed.

I started massaging her legs. She tried to stop me but I kept doing it out of sheer habit. Amma was quiet, and I waited for her to speak. The room was dark but there was light on Amma's forehead. I had a sudden and incredible idea. Is Amma on the same side as Sangita? I could not decide why I could have such a thought about Amma. Was this an indication of my real nature? Had I begun to suspect everyone because of my fear of losing Sangita? Unaware of all these thoughts flitting through my head, Amma was giving me her blessings. We were, as it were, two different ports being washed by two different sets of ocean waves.

Amma gestured to me to stop pressing her legs. I stopped, and waited for her to speak but she remained quiet. I traced the circles and squares on the sheet with my fingers. I would occasionally glance at Amma's face, full of light and a mysterious silence. Had she fallen asleep?

'Amma,' I said, chasing away the silence.

'Hmmm...' She was wide awake.

Unlike other old people, Amma enjoyed most things about modern times. She did not complain.

'Does she say anything about me?' I could not control myself any longer.

'Turn on the light, it's getting dark.'

She did not hear me. Deliberately? I wondered.

I went to the switch board and turned on the button but the tube light did not come on. I turned it off, then on again. I got the stool from the next room and climbing it, turned the starter, then the tube, and it came on after a few false starts.

'She calls every day,' Amma said as I sat down. 'She keeps a check on my medicines.'

When I raised the topic of the encounter with Dr Aditya, she already knew about it. She gave Sukhjot chachi a scolding for having told me. She said that women should not tell men such things. Women are completely capable of dealing with them themselves. To bring a man into it is to make a mountain out of a molehill. The man will pester his own woman with questions: why did this happen with you, of all people? You will be like the man who simply went to say his *namaz* prayers, and was in turn ordered to perform more *roza* fasts. Amma explained all this.

'Panna fell ill just a week ago,' Amma told me about Papa. 'There was no one at home. I tried to call you.' Amma put her hand on my shoulder, seeing my surprise. 'It's useless to phone Rinku and Suman for anything…their jobs are such. Chiku had taken Meena to her family.' Amma was now sitting up. She cleared her throat and spat into the spittoon. 'Then I phoned Sangita and she was here in 15 minutes…you know it's her eighth month…still.' Amma's eyes were full of gratitude and blessings.

'My Sangita is so courageous. You have not understood her, Masterji.' It was like a mild slap, of love and encouragement.

'Is it true, Amma, that I have not been able to understand her?' I was injured.

I would have been neither worried nor pained had someone else said it, but Amma's statement came from 60 years of experience and wisdom.

'No, no. Your heart is as transparent as water. Of course, you understand her.' Amma fondly ran her fingers through my hair. 'I am only talking about that quality of hers to love and sacrifice.'

'The fool,' I scolded Sangita in my mind. I'm not sure whether it was with love or annoyance. If she wanted to have nothing to do with me, why was she being so caring and devoted to my family?

I thought back of the furnace-hot afternoon in June. Her curt 'no' to me. Her dryness. My phoning her about the conflict with a fellow doctor. Her scolding, indifferent, violent voice. Everything. The bitterness of the past three months all came back. And here was another Sangita. Maybe she wanted me to feel inferior. Maybe she wanted my family to feel even more ashamed in front of her.

I loved her, and was also angry with her.

'Did she ever say anything about me?' I was full of curiosity.

'She had had the divorce papers made by the lawyer,' Amma said, looking at me keenly. Her voice was gentle again as she added, 'She was sending them for you to sign. I stopped her, asked her to think it over once more, but she wouldn't listen. Then she phoned some days later to say that she had not sent them.

'Why?' I remembered Ayesha's words. Had she met Sangita at this point?

'I don't know. She was saying that a relationship comes from the heart, and when the heart becomes indifferent, what is the value of a piece of paper. I advised her that day that if she wanted to continue her relationships with people, she should overlook their mistakes, and if she wanted to break her relationships, she should search for their mistakes.

'She is stubborn.' I could not contain myself.

'No…she is self-respecting,' Amma's voice spoke firmly in Sangita's favour. 'Any self-respecting woman should do as she is doing.'

'Amma…I am yours…' I became tearful.

'She is also mine,' Amma's firmness became more unsympathetic.

I could not say anything after this. Amma could not either. We became like strangers to each other.

The unspoken became like a huge web around us, through which filtered some voices and came to us. Amma had strange sides to her. I came back home.

Time did not fly, as it sometimes does, with wings that are soundless. Instead, time was like a mouse trembling at death's door, caught in the jaws of a cat.

Sangita's rejection hurt, and the darts of hundreds of memories of her made deep wounds.

CHAPTER TWENTY ONE

Banwarilal

'When even two fruits from the same branch of a tree are not the same in looks and flavour, how can the millions of people of a caste or religion be all the same?' I said, at the end of my patience.

He had been trying for the past hour to bring me to 'the correct path'. He wanted to turn me against Firoz. He wanted me to drop him from the hospital project and not let him marry Vaishali. He claimed that Firoz was greedy and untrustworthy.

I knew that chacha was not only anti-Muslim but also anti-Jatav, and deep inside, anti-Brahmin. The anti-Muslim attitude was recent, developed after his joining some Hindutva group. Such born-again Hindus show even more fervour than born-again Muslims. Chacha ji was one such, who at the drop of a hat wailed the Hindutva chant, 'Every child belongs to Rama, every child must work for Rama's birthplace.'

He was, in fact, an emotional person. I considered sadhus, mafia members and emotional people the most selfish. They are weak, and perhaps their weakness leads to their extreme selfishness.

He did not want to work for Khatiks either. He could only work and die for himself, so anyone who could abet him in this was his friend. If he had been a Muslim, there would have been no truer Muslim than him, fighting for his pure identity against all Hindus and non-Muslims.

I was not surprised at chachaji's unannounced arrival. It was natural. I knew we were being watched. Those in power, and those behind those in power, were keeping a watch on every little movement of ours. This was their work and their duty. Chacha ji had been directed to us from an invisible but powerful centre of authority.

'But a guava tree does not bear apples. You might have seen such a tree but Banwarilal hasn't,' he gestured with his hands and neck.

'It is impossible for me to drop Firoz.' I found it best to answer him briefly, now that he had descended to illogicality. I could have done that before and saved us one hour. But it would have been dictatorial.

Giving a hearing to our opponents should not be taboo. I talked to him for so long because of the belief that our opponents should have the freedom to talk.

'You are just a child, my boy. Banwari knows this type well. They committed such heinous acts on our women at the time of Partition. They even cut off the breasts of our women,' as he said this, his mouth widened, his eyebrows rose and his nostrils flared.

He kept saying other assorted things. He knew all his dialogues pat, and he was using his body to make his talk more persuasive. It was all useless, however. While he was talking, I looked at the calendar and planned the rest of the programme for the remaining days. I smiled at the child on the calendar with his tongue sticking out in fun. Then I tried to imagine myself in chachaji's place and him, in mine. I looked at the darkening sky outside and hoped he would leave soon. I thought of Sangita once or twice, and of Ayesha about 10 times. I was kicking myself for the moment when I had told him I was free. Now I could only keep quiet to dissuade him from further talk. I found it extraordinary that he knew about Vaishali and Firoz's wedding. That was a secret known to only a few people.

'Were you around at the time of Partition?' I could not restrain myself. In spite of my vow to keep quiet, his stupid words were provocative. I realised that his age was not more than 40 to 45.

'Is it necessary to have seen the Partition fighting? Don't we see and hear about fighting in riots every day? Is everyone as blind as you are?' he descended to abuses, taking an unfair advantage of his age and relationship.

'Do they ever sit still?' he was aroused by my words. 'Hindus are peaceful and patient.'

'And you are a Hindu?' I could not stop myself from asking.

I knew that when the greatest minds in the nation had failed in defining Hinduism, this little mouse could hardly succeed.

'Yes, Banwarilal is a Hindu…Repeat with pride that we are Hindus,' he made a fist and shouted the slogan.

The darkness outside was creeping in.

'And Jatavs and Valmikis?' I built up a preface to my point.

'Just call them the Chuhras and Chamars…they are Harijans,' his voice had revulsion.

'So, they are not Hindus.'

'They are, but of low ranks…other kinds of Hindus,' he said indifferently.

'So, you must be of the same rank as Brahmins and Thakurs?'

'No, they are higher than us…we are the masses,' he sounded happy to surrender.

'That is, you are a Harijan in their eyes,' I looked at him.

I thought of the village of Lalpur Khurd and, its chief, Bharatiram. Bharatiram was a Balai, and called Valmikis Harijans.

Chachaji had turned red. I recognised it. 'Am I not right, the castes below them are Harijans?'

'What?' he said as if waking up from a sleep. 'No, I am not a Harijan.'

'Then how can any caste be Harijan?' My statements were fluent and dispassionate, but clearly one-sided. 'All right, tell me this. If these castes are Hindus, then why do other Hindus act like their enemies, and attack their property and women just as they do those of non-Hindus. Father Staines, Babri Masjid, Godhra, does it ring a bell?'

'Muslims have castes too,' he repeated like a trained parrot.

'Then have they, like Hindus, done violence to the property or women of other Muslims?' I had decided to finally shut him up. 'Tell me if they are violent among themselves like Hindus? And don't we know that their castes are also India's contribution?'

'But brother,' his voice had a trace of calmness on his pronouncing 'brother', 'a Hindu family could not stay in a Muslim neighbourhood in peace, the way a Muslim family could in a Hindu neighbourhood.' His voice had become gentle now, as if he had mentally decided on surrender.

I could easily have given him an answer to this, indeed with great exegesis. The answer was that Hindus were themselves not united like Muslims were. To be 'Muslim' was an identity In a way that 'Hindu' was not. There were, rather, Brahmins, Thakurs, Baniyas, Kayasthas, Valmikis, Jatavs, Khatiks, Kolis, Nais, Kurmis and Ahirs. 'Hindu' was an artificially created association of different and almost antagonistic identities.

The many tribes within the association called 'Hinduism' each had their own gods. They worshipped their own gods and habitually disliked the gods and rituals of the others. In spite of now being knit together in a large association, they had not succeeded in forgetting their old habits. Apart from the Shaivites,

Vaishnavites, and Shaktas, hundreds of smaller groups with their gods and rituals had been pushed into this association. They are still disunited as a result, and their tolerance is hardly tolerance, it is their compulsion. A bitter truth…Two families of Brahmins will be living in a Jat village in as alienated a way as two Hindu families in a Muslim neighbourhood.

'The minority always gets a beating, so in front of the dominant group, it keeps its fangs out and its tail in,' is all I could say to chachaji. Sometimes your annoyance makes you limited in articulation.

I knew he would get my meaning. He had complained about his fellow-Khatiks once to me. There were fewer people of his Mahaman gotra of Khatiks in his village, and more of the Sejwal gotra. So, every council decision was controlled by the Sejwals, and their preferences ruled.

We found nothing further to say after this. After a long silence, I put on the lights and arranged my books on the table.

'Banwarilal will take your leave, brother,' he said, and pressed down on his knees to get up. His words fell heavily between us. He moved towards the door; I swiftly opened it.

'Where should I go, brother, to which dark well?' he muttered at the door.

I said, 'See you, chachaji,' and he turned and smiled…a defeated, hopeless smile.

CHAPTER TWENTY TWO

The 'Others'

Trrri-i-i-ng...the phone was ringing inside. I looked mechanically at the screen for the number; it was Sushil calling.

'Where did you disappear, idiot?' Sushil's roar could be heard.

'That uncle of mine just licked my brains clean. I went to see him off outside. What's up?' I massaged my forehead with my other hand.

'What was he saying?' Sushil was familiar with uncle's casteist proclivities.

'He was talking about Firoz, how we should not trust Muslims,' I knocked my forehead with my fist.

'Not Muslims…we should not trust Chamars,' he was laughing, but I could sense that he was in the grips of some tense thoughts.

'Please, Sushil, don't you start. Why did you phone?' I decided to stick to the point.

'You've made the website for our NGO, haven't you?' came the voice from the other side.

'Yes,' I answered briefly.

'Yes, pal. Dalits can progress only through technology,' came the voice again.

'Right.' After a few seconds I added, 'Anything else?'

'You've phoned everyone?' came the voice again.

'Yes.' I was afraid that to talk more would lead to tiresome arguments like before. He was asking about the plan for laying the foundation of our infants' hospital and crèche on 14th October. It was on 14 October 1956 that Baba Saheb Ambedkar had taken off his old religion as if it was old clothes, and put on new ones.

That day marked the biggest conversion in the known history of the world.

'I wanted to say something to you for many days.'

'Speak.'

'I don't want Jayant...He is a good person, I like him, in spite of our differences...but pressure is being put on me.' Sushil was speaking in disconnected pieces as if he was very reluctant to speak.

'What do you want to say Sushil?' I asked impatiently.

'I don't want any Chamar to be in this project.' Now there was a whiff of repulsion, jealousy, anger.

'They will push us in a corner every time by the sheer

strength of their numbers,' he replied. 'They will never give us leadership,' he added when he saw that I was silent.

'And you would give it?'

'I? I'm only worried about my people,' his voice came after a lot of heavy breathing. 'Should they be allowed to die out without a fight…helpless, weak…I am being pressurised… When we try to act for our caste, these same people call us "casteist" and talk about Dalit unity. But the truth is that these people are against our independent existence and want to make us serve their own caste. Otherwise, why did they never think of doing anything for our caste? We were the ones always running around for them. You can pretend to not understand all this and to keep dreaming of Dalit unity…I can't.' His broken voice was breaking up my dreams to pieces.

'Are we all separate then?' I was shocked at his speech. What was going on? Why had he been reduced to thinking like this? How did it come to this? I put the question to him.

'Yes…we are one but also not one.'

A silence engulfed us after this, like a python getting ready to swallow.

'Wait and see…this conflict will only grow…tomorrow it will be between the Chamars of western Uttar Pradesh. That's why I want to draw this border between us today itself,' he unburdened himself in one breath.

'You have been misled, Sushil…maybe by some old-time thinkers…this is neither wise nor possible…all right, see you,' I disconnected the phone without waiting for his yes or no.

Friendships cannot last when friends get into such an unequivocal tussle. They break down sooner or later.

But why am I giving so much importance to any Banwarilal, Sushil or anyone else?

This was but a clash of egos and personal ambitions. In the infatuation with all these ideas, the powerful and entrenched could not see clearly those people who were lying unseen in the dust of the villages, being killed and burnt there. These were not Valmikis, or Jatavs, or Musahars, or Dusadhs, not even Mahar, Madiga or Dhanuk—they were only oppressed people…they were only powerless people who could not defend themselves.

The powerful people were searching for the exact caste identities of the powerless!

CHAPTER TWENTY THREE

Maya Arrives

The days were breaking off and melting into one, just as a river is formed from a glacier breaking up.

It was the 14th of October. A day same as others. There was the same morning outside and the same melancholy sunlight inside, but there was a new thrill in the mind that set the day apart. It was a festival, or perhaps a festival of the mind. A kind of sunlight from the mind was casting its rays on the whole room and the whole of creation.

We all reached village Rajpur Khurd by 10. Sushil, Jayant, Vedprakash, Papa, Chiku, Aslam, Rajbir, Sudesh Chacha and Sukhjot Chachi, Bharatiram ji, Dr Baney Singh, Master Ramratan Sharma, Ratiram and his son Dhaniram, the MLA Dr Sukhdev Singh Tanwar—all had gathered.

Who would lay the foundation stone? The question became a ball tossed around by the group. Everyone named the other but everyone was perhaps thinking about themselves. As someone was named, his appropriateness for the action was described. The named person then, with theatrical humility, counted out his shortcomings and described as more suited someone else, or the person who had named him. This continued for over half an hour. The responsibility for the foundation stone passed from my shoulders to Sushil, Jayant, Firoz, Papa and the MLA, and each one shrugged it off.

'Ask Priyanka's mother to do it,' said the soft voice of Master Ramratan Sharma.

He was sitting between me and Sushil. He spoke so softly that only the two of us heard it, with difficulty.

'Let Priyanka's mother do it, Pradhanji,' Sushil said.

'Absolutely,' said Jayant, sitting in front.

'Absolutely, absolutely,' everyone agreed. It was an unprecedented idea, but everyone's countenance expressed agreement with it. The MLA, Dr Sukhdev Singh Tanwar, was accepting it with a downcast look. He was a politician, always aware of his status.

Did Master Ramratan Sharma give the suggestion deliberately so that the opportunity to lay the foundation stone would not go to a politician who was a Jat by caste, and had nothing to do with the work?

Whatever it was, it was a humanitarian suggestion, and therefore, appropriate.

'Listen, listen, gentlemen, listen.'

Pradhan Bharatiram put on his Chief's hat now and then. Before him were us, Master Ramratan Sharma, and distinguished Jats. He had nothing to fear from us but did have something to fear from the others. There was silence.

'Speak up, Bharati, speak up. What do you want to say?' Ratiram said this as a scold, which is how he talked to everyone. He even called the MLA not by name, but as the son of his, the MLA's, father.

'Yes, Chaudhuri sahab, but she has become insane, meaning—half-mad,' Bharatiram rotated his forefinger near his head to show his meaning.

'Not half-mad, but completely....' came a villager's voice.

'Yes sir, she does go out to work, but after Priyanka's death...' Bharatiram's voice had fear, or respect, or respect born out of fear, but whatever it was, he was unable to speak clearly.

The judgement on a slave itself extends the slave-like status.

'Never mind. Send someone to call her. This is her right,' Ratiram's voice had changed. It was a new Ratiram, not the one who had been talking to the villagers and the MLA just now.

Everyone was whispering among themselves. Time was passing. As the sun rose, people drifted towards the shade of trees.

I looked at my watch and saw that it was a quarter to twelve. The sky was unexpectedly clear, completely clear. This was the sky of our capital city...so clear.

Dr Baney Singh sent a boy to call Rupa, then followed him. Sushil began to talk about Priyanka and her mother Rupa.

Jayant and Papa were talking among themselves; Rinku stood nearby. The MLA sat with his legs crossed, sometimes one leg over the other, sometimes the reverse. Master Ramratan Sharma and Chaudhuri Ratiram sat on the rug and spoke softly. Chief Bharatiram, sitting nearby, was vehemently agreeing with everything they said.

The scenes kept shifting as someone entered or left a scene. The whole thing was a collage of shifting scenes.

Just like life.

My mobile's ring put an end to my observation. The screen showed 'Papa'. That meant the call was coming from home.

'Hello,' I switched on my phone.

'Yes, Masterji, I am Amma speaking,' came Amma's voice.

'Yes, Amma. Is everything all right?' My voice was worried. I was fed up with this habit of mine, of getting worried.

'Sangita has just gone to the hospital...we got a call,' Amma told me.

I became restless. There was fear, melting away, there was delight, exploding. I moved towards where Papa, Jayant and Chiku were standing with the phone in my ear. They were talking and paying no attention to me.

'Papa, Sangita has been taken to the Indian Ayurvigyan Hospital, Amma just called to say,' I informed him.

'You go along, we'll handle it here,' Jayant said uncertainly.

'No, you wait, Masterji…Chiku and I will go. You wrap up the work here and then come,' said Papa, and took out money from his pocket and counted it. I immediately took out my purse and put 10 notes of 500 in his hand. 'Chiku, how much do you have?'

'Only about a thousand. I did not think of bringing any,' Chiku's voice was helpless.

'That's fine. I have 2,200,' he murmured. 'About 8,000 altogether. That should be enough,' he calculated.

'Keep this, too, uncle,' Jayant had taken out some five 100-rupee notes.

'No, no, don't. If we need more, I'll send Chiku home to get some,' assured Papa, moving ahead. He didn't take the money though Jayant offered it another two or three times. 'The labour must have just begun; it's going to take time.' He saw the stress on my face. He patted my shoulders, told me not to worry and gave me the solace of constant phone calls from there.

I wanted to fly there if I could.

'Rupa has gone to Beldari with her husband,' Dr Baney Singh came and delivered the news.

We were back to square one.

'The MLA is requested to launch this important work with his hands,' Sushil announced. He, Jayant, Firoz, Bharatiram and I had meanwhile conferred and come to this decision. We were now keen to finish up as soon as possible.

'No…no, sir,' the MLA kept refusing, but while his tongue said no, his moustache smiled in acceptance. His eyes laughed and his forehead beamed. Finally, under everyone's pressure, with a 'Whatever the people decide!', he performed the ceremony.

We left for the hospital shortly after. Firoz, Aslam, Jayant and Bharatiram were with me. Father was sitting on the chair outside the Delivery Room. Meena was inside with Sangita. Mother was at the end of the row of chairs, her back turned, eating. Chiku had gone for the medications the doctor had ordered.

The scene changed.

Chiku had delivered the things and was resting on the chairs. Meena was saying something to him in his ear. Mother was not in the scene. Father was walking up and down in the verandah. Firoz, Aslam and Jayant were standing and talking. Bharatiram stood on my right and smoked a *bidi*. Vedprakash had joined the scene.

The scenes kept changing further.

'It's a girl,' said mother, coming out, to father.

Mother's voice was like an experienced diplomat. She was neither happy nor sad. She was neutral. Everyone was congratulating me. I had become a father.

'My little daughter…thank you,' said my heart inside me.

Bharatiram's voice was like mother's: neutral. Everyone else was leaping with joy.

'She is asking for you, Masterji,' Amma's voice pierced my consciousness.

The scene had changed again. Everyone had left. I had fallen asleep on a chair. Mother's place was taken by Amma.

Amma sat down on a nearby chair. I looked at the clock. It was 7:00. The hospital verandah was as crowded, only the people were different. Some had left, some had come, and some were the same as in the afternoon, and were perhaps getting ready to leave. Where to? Was this how life was? Why?

I looked at Amma. She was sitting back restfully in her chair, her eyes closed.

Was a change in expression the only difference between life and death? There was an immense peace on her fair, wrinkled face, as the water in a deep mountain stream is calm and peaceful. His hair and eyebrows were as white as snow. Wrapped in a brown shawl, my aged Amma looked to me like a newborn child.

Tomorrow, I will be sitting in her place in the same circumstances. I liked her immense peace. Would I be able to achieve this peace as well? Has the peace been born out of a meaningful life? What was Amma's great achievement? I was thrashing around in a web of thoughts. The more I tried to force myself to escape, the more I was getting caught. I was like an elephant trapped in a swamp.

In an instant, in a one-hundredth part of that moment, I suddenly knew. I let myself be open to the moment. I was saved.

'You are still here.' Amma arose, took my hand, and led me into the room.

Sangita was in a bed in the third room, which we reached after crossing two. Her eyes were closed. But she was not my Sangita. She was someone else. Had she changed so completely simply by becoming a mother? Has something changed inside me as well? What was this new sensation within me, and why was it?

Sangita was lying there, her eyes closed.

'Sit down.' Amma sat down on a stool near the bed. She gestured to another stool. She had said 'Sit down' with her eyes.

Just as I got ready to sit, my phone vibrated. I had put it on silent on entering the hospital. Rana's name appeared on the screen.

'What bad timing,' I thought and wanted to reject the call but did not.

'Yes, Rana,' I took long steps and reached outside the room.

'Sorry, pal. I could not come…something came up at the office,' his voice was cordial.

'It's all right. Everything is over. I am in the hospital,' I said impatiently.

'Everything is well?' his voice sounded worried.

'Yes, all is well...I've become a father. A daughter has come to my house.'

'Wow, great...congratulations!' his voice was enthusiastic. 'It's a good day, Professor, I am congratulating people, there is happiness all around...You know that Kalra has decided to marry, some widow lady...he was giving you the credit,' his voice sounded pleased.

'Congratulations from me; right, we'll meet soon.' As soon as he said okay, I cut the phone.

I returned to the room. Amma was stroking Sangita's forehead. Sangita's eyes were still closed, like a small child's. Maybe she was sleeping. My eyes went to the blue scarf tied on her head. It was a gift from me on our second meeting.

Suddenly, Sangita opened her eyes. Could she feel that someone was staring at her? She was looking directly at me, and in that look, there was recognition. She was looking at the father of her child. She was looking at her husband. 'We're complete now,' I said, advancing.

Sangita took out her hand from the blanket and moved back the blanket a little. My child lay there...eyes closed, lost in a sweet dream, my little squirrel, my little fair doll...my very breath. Her dark and silky-soft hair were spread on her forehead. She was pale; she had inherited Sangita's complexion.

'She will look like you,' Amma said, watching me observe her.

I was still standing. I was unable to go further as if my hands were chained. I was smiling at the little reflection of me. I was watching the future in the present.

'A man and a woman may fall apart easily, Masterji,' Amma said, getting up. She understood my inability to move. 'A mother and a father cannot fall apart so easily.'

My aged Amma, slowly, with small steps, toddling like a child, left the room. Her old, dark eyes had rained blessings on us.

My daughter opened her eyes, as if to say, 'Greetings...welcome!' She was looking with innocent surprise, unblinking.

'Amma…her name?' I called after Amma, who had reached the door.

'She is your Maya, Masterji,' Amma paused and emphasised, 'Maya.'

'Can we look at life like you, with mere surprise, Maya?' I moved her hair away from her forehead with my forefinger.

'Can we actually do nothing more than that?' I murmured, but distinctly. I opened her closed fist gently.

'Here, too!' I murmured again. She had a mark at the heel of her thumb, near the wrist, a little fly-shaped mark.

'Sa-a-a-b, should I take away the garbage?' I turned around. Sangita had gestured to my back with her hand on mine.

A lady with white gloves and a scarf around her mouth was standing at the door. She was looking at the dustbin near the stool.

'So many worlds within one world!' Maya's fist curled around my finger.

The question on Sangita's face became a smile.

The scene changed yet again.

Caste Terms and Their Relationships

Jatav is a sub-caste of the Chamar community and comes under the Scheduled Caste category, officially. They are mainly residents of the western part of Uttar Pradesh. Ancestrally, they were associated with agricultural and leather work.

Mahar is a caste and comes under the Scheduled Caste category, officially. They are concentrated in Maharashtra, but are also residents of Karnataka and Andhra Pradesh. Ancestrally, they were associated with agricultural work.

Chamar is a caste which comes under the Scheduled Caste category, officially. They are largely concentrated in the northern parts of India. Ancestrally, they were associated with the work of tanning, making of leather goods and also worked as agricultural help on farms.

Valmiki is a caste which comes under the Scheduled Caste category, officially. They are largely concentrated in the northern parts of India. Ancestrally, they were associated with manual scavenging and cleaning of villages.

Bhangi is a caste which comes under the Scheduled Caste category, officially. They are largely concentrated in the northern parts of India. They are ancestrally associated with the work of manual scavenging and cleaning of villages. From about the 20th century, the term 'Valmiki' has been used synonymously for the Bhangi caste.

Khatik is a caste which comes under Scheduled Caste category, and in some states under Other Backward Class category, officially. They are mainly residents of Rajasthan, Punjab, Haryana, Delhi, Uttar Pradesh, Madhya Pradesh and Andhra Pradesh. Their ancestral occupations were hunting, agricultural farming and selling fruits, vegetables and goat-meat.

Dom is a caste which comes under the Scheduled Caste category, officially. They are mainly concentrated in Bengal, Bihar and eastern parts of Uttar Pradesh. They are ancestrally associated with the work of cremation and cleaning of villages.

Balai is a caste which comes under the Scheduled Caste category, officially. They are mainly concentrated in Rajasthan and Delhi. They are ancestrally associated with the work of weaving, but in some states they are also associated with leatherwork.

Acknowledgements

Ordinarily, when engaged in a challenging work such as this translation, one would have presented the analytical parts at this or that academic venue, and received the useful feedback of colleagues. Covid-19 took care of that. This whole translation was done in total isolation, away from the academy, literally on the banks of the Ganga.

I have, therefore, to give extra thanks to family members who made such a sojourn not only possible but progressively more comfortable and exciting. My daughter and colleague, Irfana Majumdar, set up a beautiful apartment for me in Betawar village, outside Varanasi, together with *my* type of desk, armchair, lamps, windows and bookshelves. She left me with no alibi for flagging in my work, and removed any possible disorientation in my sudden move to a village. The intense political consciousness of Gaurav Saini, my son-in-law, was hugely stimulating; he was always ready with questions or responses. My granddaughter Samira made life beautiful.

We had the leisure to wear matching clothes, and to design different parts of our lives. Nandini Majumdar, my younger daughter, was not there but is an academic who works on Dalit voices, among other things. Far away in Austin, Texas, she read parts of the manuscript as it progressed.

In this case, there was also an experience of interacting with staff members of the organisation I support, NIRMAN. Together, we created a world of farming, planting, cooking, learning, playing and talking together (at a suitable distance) that can only be envied.

Translating the novel was a project that was like therapy in troubled times. My thanks to the publishers, especially Nirmal Kanti Bhattacharjee, and my editor, Vibha Chakravarty Kumar, for seeing it through to completion.

Nita Kumar